MOBILE

THE A
PORTABLE
ARCHITECTURE

# MOBILE

# THE ART OF PORTABLE ARCHITECTURE

EDITED BY
JENNIFER SIEGAL
FOREWORD BY ANDREI CODRESCU
PREFACE BY ROBERT KRONENBURG

**PRINCETON ARCHITECTURAL PRESS** I NEW YORK

Published by
Princeton Architectural Press
37 East Seventh Street
New York, New York 10003

For a free catalog of books, call 1.800.722.6657.
Visit our web site at www.papress.com.

Printed in Hong Kong
05 04 03    5 4 3 2

Project editing: Clare Jacobson
Text editing: Beth Harrison
Editorial assistance: Nicola Bednarek
Design: Jan Haux

Special thanks to: Nettie Aljian, Ann Alter, Janet Behning,
Penny Chu, Jan Cigliano, Mark Lamster, Nancy Eklund Later,
Linda Lee, Evan Schoninger, Jane Sheinman, Lottchen Shiv-
ers, Scott Tennent, Katharine Smalley, Jennifer Thompson,
and Deb Wood of Princeton Architectural Press
—Kevin C. Lippert, publisher

Library of Congress Cataloging-in-Publication Data
Mobile: the art of portable architecture / Jennifer Siegal,
editor; foreword by Andrei Codrescu; preface by Robert
Kronenburg.
p. cm.
Includes bibliographical references.
ISBN 1-56898-334-4
1. Buildings, Portable. 2. Lightweight construction. I. Siegal,
Jennifer, 1965–
NA8480.M598 2002
720'.4—dc21                              2002000854

All images courtesy of the contributors unless otherwise noted.

page 002: Office of Mobile Design.

page 008: Collection Office of Mobile Design.

page 010: Allan D. Wallis, *Wheel Estate* (New York: Oxford
University Press, 1991), p. 54.

page 012: George McKay, *Senseless Acts of Beauty* (London:
Verso, 1996), p. 37.

page 015: Jim Burns, *Arthropods: New Design Futures*
(New York: Praeger Publishers, 1971), p. 133.

Every reasonable attempt has been made to identify owners
of copyright. Errors or omissions will be corrected in subse-
quent editions.

# CONTENTS

ANDREI
CODRESCU:
FOREWORD

ROBERT KRONENBURG:
PREFACE

JENNIFER SIEGAL: THE AGE
OF NEW NOMADISM

Hot-dog vendor, Coney Island,
New York, 1968

In memory of my grandfather, Abraham Lederman, a mobile
entrepreneur.

## ACKNOWLEDGEMENTS

Clare Jacobson, my editor, for her devotion to her craft.

Princeton Architectural Press, for sharing in and giving shape to my vision.

The fluid members of Office of Mobile Design: Elmer Barco, Jon Racek, Ashley Moore, Thao Nguyen, Arona Witte, Greg Roth, and Lori Jay.

Geraldine Forbes, for her steadfast belief, and Woodbury University, for the institutional support.

My former design/build students at Woodbury University, during the spring and summer of 1998, whose boundless passions for the work continue to inspire me.

Todd Erlandson (building), Robert Gonzalez (theory), and Bill Brunner (provocateur), for their collaborative encouragement.

Benny Chan, my friend and photographer of all built Office of Mobile Design work.

Mostly, I acknowledge and thank deeply my family—Gail, Steven, Richard, and Sidney Siegal—for inspiration, love, and support.

# FOREWORD

BY ANDREI CODRESCU

The Trailer of Tomorrow, designed by Carl X. Meyer in 1940 (a contemporary of Wally Byman's Airstream), features a streamlined, aerodynamic shell, the image of a bullet propelled through space.

I'm for portable houses and nomadic furniture. Anything you can't fold up and take with you is a blight on the environment, and an insult to one's liberty. I believe in the tent, the card table, and the trailer. The past two decades have witnessed a huge increase in nomadism. For every housing development that carves up the land, a flock of houses on wheels and pontoons takes off somewhere else. Where is the great literature of the mobile home, the trailer park, the perpetual camper, the floating boathouse?

American society has become mobile, yet it still depends, for the most part, on stationary dwellings. But while stationary, most new American houses are impermanent. Although a house in a subdivision is not portable, it is certainly interchangeable with any other house in any other subdivision—and the subdivisions themselves often evaporate. This evaporation is sometimes brought about by company relocations, or by the city moving closer to what was once almost country. Quite often, suburbs become the abodes of new immigrants who have come to America in search of stability, after leaving behind old houses that will long outlive their new homes. The house in Sibiu, Romania, where I was born, was built in the seventeenth century and still stands. Nearly every American house I've lived in has long ago been demolished to make room for some other building. There is a delicious (though painful) paradox here: Americans long for stability, but all they get is stationary impermanence. No wonder, then, that many of us long to become permanent nomads, snails with houses on our backs, Touareg tribesmen, and Gypsies.

We certainly cannot indulge in nostalgia for home, because most American houses are not homes. Grown-ups will rarely revisit the places where they grew up because nothing remains of their first home, their grade school, or their tree house. The nuclear family has long ago scattered, buying new houses every few years, always putting down shallow roots. Paradoxically, again, then, a moving house becomes more permanent than a stationary house, and a better means of keeping connections between family members and thus a sense of rootedness: In your mobile dwelling you can visit your family all the time.

Today, the workplace is moving into the home, thanks to decentralizing computer technology. A new definition of the house is in the works. Once an exclusively domestic domain, the house of the future will have to allow for work. There will be no escape in the work-connected house from paging devices, telephones, and surveillance equipment. The predictions of science-fictioneers will doubtlessly come true: The house will become a work-farm prison with limited opportunities for escape. Since everyone will then always be at home, what is the point of keeping the house in one place? It will matter little where the plugged-in house is. Since it is always present in the global, decentralized hyperspace of function, its location will be irrelevant. You can take your physical reality practically anywhere, without fear of losing either your job or your community. You will always encounter new people and visit old friends.

A long time ago, the word "house" was the best argument for the impossibility of translation. An American house was not a French *maison* or a Spanish *casa*, which was evident to anyone who'd been inside a Mediterranean villa or a walled-in Moorish *casa* in Cádiz. Houses embodied local culture more than anything else, even more than human beings themselves. Humans adapted more easily to new conditions and had more "universal" mechanisms than houses, which, in their commitment to geography, weather, history, and the humans who lived in them, were utterly and wholly specific. This will no longer be the case in our global, decentralized, portable world. You will be able to transport your skeuomorphs, younostalgias, and your roots to wherever you wish.

Inspired by the 1960s American counter culture, the Albion truck at Sun Fair, Lyng, 1980, bridges the cultures of resistance from hippie to punk.

BY ROBERT KRONENBURG

# PREFACE

It is in our genes to be nomadic. For nearly all of human-kind's history, just to survive we have found it necessary to live our lives on the move. As the enduring protohuman species, *Homo sapiens* followed a hunter-gatherer existence, shifting "home" from place to place as required by the demands of hunger and climate. This movement was often seasonal and a pattern, but the flexibility and adaptability it engendered in our species also enabled much bigger geographic shifts to take place as environmental change and natural disasters made regions of the earth uninhabitable.

In the last ten thousand years most of us have settled down somewhat, and become used to farmed food delivered to the centers of commerce and industry that have become our cities. However, some groups of people never stopped moving. On every continent there are traditional cultures that have refused to respond to the sometimes extreme pressures to take up a sedentary lifestyle. Without doubt it is their traditions, their culture, their identity that they seek to retain—but it is their mobile buildings that have made it possible for them to keep moving, and to stay connected to their ancestry. As they were in their forebears' time, these buildings are still made by the people who use them, to patterns developed over thousands of generations, and are still able to accommodate the exigencies of life on the move. Such mobile structures are the pattern book that inspired the permanent architectural forms in which most of us now live, and they still hold lessons for contemporary design in their economic, lightweight, flexible approach to providing shelter.

Now it seems that a return to mobile living is imminent for many more of us. In North America, it is a common phenomenon for retired people, released from the burden of a lifetime's work, to sell the house, buy a trailer home, and become "snowbirds." Moving between the fixed homes of their children and grandchildren, they follow the clement weather from north to south in a migratory pattern similar in effect, if not in ethos or style, to that of the native Americans who inhabited this landscape for the thousands of years before the immigrant nation was formed.

The change is being brought about by the information age, which has made it possible for many of us who are still immersed in the world of work to also seek out a mobile life. Within a week of writing this piece I will begin a three-month, round-the-world journey of more than twenty two thousand miles. Though I have some stopping points identified, I have few other details about these locations and no set itinerary. But with my Apple iBook computer (which weighs less than five pounds) and my Motorola Timeport tri-band mobile phone (just four ounces), I will be able to connect instantly to all the people I work with, obtain data on almost anything I care to find out about, make travel and accommodation arrangements, manage my finances, and buy almost anything and have it waiting for me wherever and whenever I arrive.

That is fine for me, an individual, with my relatively limited needs, making use of the buildings erected for similar travelers. While my physical needs for food and shelter are conventional, however, many human activities are not so simple, concerning various-sized groups of people often undertaking complex activities—commerce, education, manufacturing, health care, and entertainment, to name just a few.

Now there is an ever-increasing need for these functions to be more flexible and adaptable, in both application and location, than they have ever been in the past. To be ultimately flexible and ultimately adaptable these activities must be sheltered by mobile architecture. Are architects and designers ready for this challenge? The answer, it would seem, is yes—because for decades they have been exposed to the potential of the portable environment. In the 1950s, 1960s, and 1970s it was the work of high-profile experimenters like Buckminster Fuller, Archigram, and the Metabolists. More recently there has been a spate of live projects for real clients with real problems, which have proven that mobile architecture is not just something that is sometimes built in situations where there is simply no other solution. More and more, an enlightened client understands that there is a performance advantage in going mobile compared to the standard, static building solution.

The traditional building forms that have always informed our understanding of the meaning of architecture—to provide shelter, a sense of place, a mirror of cultural and societal endeavors—still inform the new mobile architecture. Tents, lightweight structural frames, and wheeled and floating structures figure in the range of recent projects. However, the possibilities of new technology are also shaping the development of the field. Pneumatic, tensile, and kinetic structures provide the opportunity for new dedicated architectural forms. Smart buildings that respond to both environmental and user demands are now being built, as are self-deploying and -erecting buildings that may remain dormant when not in use or being transported, but that change in form and volume when occupied. Perhaps most significant is that mobile architecture, which was in the recent past usually treated with contempt as the "cheap" alternative or ignored entirely in favor of temporary building solutions that are wastefully demolished when their short period of usefulness is over, is now being seen in a very different light. It is not only a forward-looking, ecologically aware alternative to permanent building, but also an experimental resource for determining the way that future permanent buildings might be made—flexible in operation and economic in the use of materials.

Mobile architecture is more than just an ephemeral solution for a temporary problem. It is a genre of building that has always been there, the prototypical human shelter that first established the human need and desire to make "home." It is linked to our definitive character as mobile beings, providing our need for stability, continuity, and a sense of place—even though that place may not be tied to a specific geographic location. With the recent advances in communications, building materials, and construction technology, mobile architecture provides new possibilities for enabling the activities associated with the sophisticated community of individuals who make up the world today. It is also updating the imagery of architecture from something built for a static, autocratic society, to something flexible, democratic, and free.

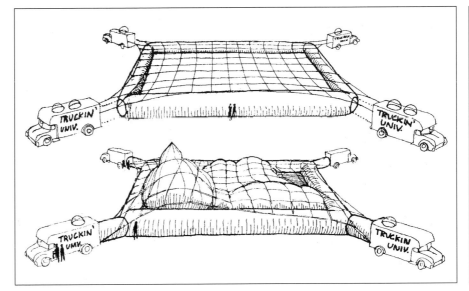

The Truckin' University, designed by Ant Farm, 1970, introduces the Pneumad, a hybrid of pneumatic and nomadic culture. This instant university is designed to be built using polyethylene, allot conduit, plastic connectors, and other cheap materials.

BY JENNIFER SIEGAL

# THE AGE OF NEW NOMADISM

The information age whets our appetite for the exploration of the unknown. As inquisitive social beings and natural explorers of the universe, we are standing at a new threshold of curiosity and movement. We are poised for more than sharing ideas over vast distances; we are ready physically to actualize these explorations. Biological and technological advancements reveal themselves in our everyday lives, echoing prophecies and environmental visions from American pulp science fiction. Architecture today rolls, flows, inflates, breathes, expands, multiplies, and contracts, finally hoisting itself up, as Archigram predicted in the early 1960s, to go in search of its next user.

While architecture's purpose remains constant—providing shelter from the natural elements and community among its inhabitants—mobile and portable structures herald the dawn of the age of new nomadism. The applications and uses are limitless; these buildings have no borders. Their material palette, design style, and transportation method are diverse. Mobile architecture, then, "can be defined not merely in terms of movable structures, but rather as a way of intelligently inhabiting a specific environment at a specific time and place in a way that better reacts to increasingly frequent social shifts."[1]

This book represents a range of creative forces behind mobile architecture today. My own interest in mobile architecture, developed at Office of Mobile Design, occurs at the intersection of portability and sustainability. As a traveler on a roving circuit of like-minded designers, architects, and engineers, I have been inspired by the work included in this volume.

Festo and its founder Alex Thallemer are the creators of Airtecture. Their buildings are comprised of supporting structures built with air-inflated chambers, taking the inflatables of the 1960s to a new stratosphere.

The atmospheric fluidity of FTL Happold's deployable and demountable tensile structures draw inspiration from the nomadic tents of the peripatetic civilizations, only these scrupulously sheathed skeletal structures develop a new vocabulary of lightness.

When Guy Debord, a member of the Situationist International, published the *Society of the Spectacle* in 1967, he was surely anticipating the work of Mark Fisher. If the "spectacle is the moment when the commodity has attained the total occupation of social life,"[2] then The Mark Fisher Studio's creations of portable touring rock shows and one-off live events—from the Rolling Stones' *Bridges to Babylon* tour to Walt Disney World—have achieved that stature.

A growing number of architects have explored the adaptive reuse of ISO shipping containers as multifunctional, all-terrain, land-and-sea, building-block solutions, both concrete and theoretical. Found in the work of LOT/EK, the MDU (Mobile Dwelling Unit) situates itself within the mobile-global dialogue of worldwide standardization and the movement toward the minimization of personal domestic artifacts. Doug Jackson of LARGE postulates

that the e-HIVE, a community of modified individual shipping container–living units that are networked both digitally and physically, will create flexible indoor/outdoor communal spaces not seen since Moshe Safdie's Habitat, built for the 1967 Montreal World's Fair. Pugh + Scarpa delve into the possibilities of the shipping container by performing surgical skin incisions and exfoliating the weathered layers, transforming the ubiquitous box into an inhabitable Picasso-esque re-rendering.

Michael A. Fox, founding director of MIT's Kinetic Design Group (KDG), explores intelligently responsive kinetic and mobile architectural systems, with primary focus on reactive spatial adaptability, multiuse applications, and automated kinetic response in regard to changing programmatic and environmental conditions. A quintessential meeting of the machine and the body, his Interactive Kinetic Facade is a 160-foot-long band of responsive "whiskers" that detect pedestrian movement and respond in a wavelike rhythm as a person walks past.

Always the aesthetic provocateur, Vito Acconci suggests in his Vehicles and Portables

that space on the run is life on the loose…in a plague year, in a time of AIDS, bodies mix while dressed in condoms and armored with vaginal shields—the body takes its own housing with it where ever it goes, it does not come out of its shell.... You come to visit, not to stay.

EVOLUTION OF A MOBILE TYPOLOGY

Historic examples of mobile architecture describe a preindustrial world not bound to place but possessed by an ideology of itinerant and nomadic responses to permanence. According to biblical history, over four thousand years ago Noah was called by God to build an ark capable of transporting the natural world and its creatures to safety when the apocalypse struck. This may have been the first portable and relocatable structure whose purpose was self-sufficient housing.

Nomadic cultures moved about for varied reasons: locating migrant food sources, adapting to changing climatic conditions, trading goods, finding communal protection, and searching for the unknown. Of these regionally disparate cultures, many shared similar challenges in their need to provide shelters that

were durable, lightweight, flexible, and ultimately transportable by low-tech means. Examples of uniquely formed tensile structures made from taut skins on supporting structures are found in the American Indian tipi, the Mongolian yurt, the Bedouin woven goat-hair "blacktent," and the Basque sheepherder tent/coat.

Not all portable structures evolved, however, out of the strict necessities of survival. As every society matures, cultural and ideological themes are expressed and relayed through public performance, art, and storytelling (often dramatized today on the Internet). In medieval Italy mystery plays, performed as populist parables drawn from biblical stories, were staged in demountable theaters called "mansiones." These platforms or booths were set up in the town marketplace or sometimes in an existing building.

Exhibitions and expositions have served as architectural petri dishes for cultivating new design ideas. Perhaps because of their temporary nature, greater risks are ventured and the wildest of dreams legitimized as genuine contributions to the furthering of building technology. In an effort to be perceived as technologically advanced, countries will display (and financially support) the otherwise unimaginable, giving shape to the hypothetical metropolis of the future. With the Great Exhibition of 1851, Great Britain provided an international forum for the display of manufacturing and industry, much like the present-day World Exposition. It was here that the way was forged for a new type of mobile building material. Joseph Paxton's Crystal Palace, built in six months during 1850–51, exploited the properties of cast-iron. The structure set a precedent for using a component system in building manufacture and site assembly and established itself on the forefront of lightweight, demountable building systems. Unlike its predecessors, "every item of the building's construction was meticulously planned for reuse in the new structure, even the temporary timber fencing was reused as floorboards inside." The system was successful in its innate logic and economy, which allowed for rapid assembly and reassembly, and could be erected in locations remote from its manufacture. The extent to which the Crystal Palace succeeded in revolutionizing the building industry or engendered a new way of building is debatable; its novelty, however, is indisputable.

Some years later, Buckminster Fuller began to work on the development of methods for producing high-quality, affordable, portable housing. Like Paxton, his primary concerns were focused on the implementation of mass production, lightness of materials, and minimal weight. His famous nonrhetorical question— "Madam, do you know what your house weighs?"—articulates a subversive suspicion of the monumental. Fuller's proposal for the Dymaxion House (dynamic-maximum-ions) was patented in 1928 and was to be built for the 1933 World's Fair. The design was influenced by technology borrowed from boat-building and the house was light enough to be transported by helicopter. If the house had been put into production in 1933 it was estimated to have cost $1,500, when the average cost for a new home in the United States was $8,000.

In 1940 Fuller designed the Mechanical Wing, which first appeared in *Architectural Forum*'s special issue "The Design Decade." As the first prototype for "plug-in" self-sufficient mobile housing, the trailer contained a compact kitchen, bathroom, and generator and was towed behind an automobile. Coupled with the Butler Bins, a circular steel container used for storing grain, the Dymaxion Deployment Unit (DDU) was the first cheap and portable dwelling, originally intended to be used for military and industrial workers' housing.

The advantages of a prefabricated system were becoming increasingly appealing: Their promise offered greater economy, speed of erection, reduction in need for skilled labor on the site, and a higher-quality product due to factory manufacture. Other designers and pioneers began investigating similar concepts. Walter Gropius and Hirsch Kupfer were engaged in the evolution of "knockdown buildings that can be easily assembled," developing and later building the Copper House in Berlin. The Berlin Growing House exhibition of 1932 showcased Gropius's design for a factory-made, flexible system that combined standardization with variability. Ray and Charles Eames already held a fascination with automated, machine-based processes in 1948 when they designed their Case Study house for editor John Entenza's *Arts and Architecture* magazine. The use of

prefabricated, commercially available products made up their palette of component pieces from which "good design" could be composed and efficiently constructed.

Premanufactured buildings have also arisen in response to various conditions of convenience or necessity. When there is a sudden, unforeseen demand and no local resources or materials, such as during natural disasters, materials are transported to a site for assembly. In 1787, Samuel Wyatt built twelve movable hospitals that could be dismantled and reerected within an hour without using tools. More recently, in the Afghanistan and the Gulf wars, portable and demountable units known as MUSTs (Medical Unit, Self-contained, Transportable) were developed by and for the military. They continue to be used around the world where speed of deployment and immediate proximity to areas of conflict are necessary.

## MOBILE MOVEMENT: FORM FOLLOWS MOBILITY

Mobile housing was a fertile playground for both practitioners and theorists throughout the twentieth century. In 1920 Le Corbusier wrote

about a French aircraft manufacturer that could easily convert its hangars to build mobile houses in Model T assembly-line fashion. Le Corbusier stated in *L'Esprit Nouveau* that it was "impossible to wait on the slow collaborations of the successive efforts of excavation, mason, carpenter, joiner, tiler, plumber.... Houses must go up all of a piece, made by machine tools in a factory, assembled as Ford assembles cars, on moving conveyer belts."

In 1937 Jean Prouvé began designing demountable structures. Having previously examined prefabricated structural systems, moveable partition walls, kiosks, rolling doors and skylights, and furniture on wheels, the J. Prouvé Workshops fabricated the prototype B.L.P.S. (Beaudouin, Lods, Prouvé, Strasbourg)

demountable house in steel, unveiled at the sixth Exposition de l'Habitation in the Salon des Arts Ménagers in January 1939. With two built-in beds, a drop-leaf table, kitchen, storage, shower, and toilet, it promised the inhabitant comfortable holiday accommodations. In one week in 1939 demountable barrack units for the Corps of Engineers were prototyped by B.L.P.S. "The first built unit was presented to the General Staff of the Engineers Corps, assembled in three hours at Birkenwald in Alsace [and] led to an immediate order of 275 examples…to be delivered during the following month."[7]

The introduction of new materials, such as ultralight fiber-based elements replacing steel, has also been key to mobile architecture's

ongoing evolution. From futuristic pure-energy plasma walls to the more tenable foam panels used for short-term, relocatable housing (e.g., for the military, migrant workers, or disaster victims), these new materials play on the ur-American concepts of progress through technology and the right to infinite mobility—the dream of being able to pack everything into the station wagon and start over from scratch.[8]

Of course America's historical precedent for the mobile dwelling was the covered or Conestoga wagon, used by the settlers heading west during the nineteenth century. Initially mass-produced for moving goods to the new frontier, the prairie schooner was quickly converted and accessorized to become a dwelling for the range-roving pioneer family. During the 1920s, when the automobile was relatively affordable, a new type of domestic-pioneer traveler began to emerge, and the pleasure of short-term travel and overnight excursions was popularized. Images such as the Aerocar Land Yacht, designed by Glenn Curtiss, combined the streamlined forms of the train and airplane to evoke a world for the independent and freedom-bound traveler. In 1936, Wally Byam's Airstream

Incorporated went into production, fostering a new dreamscape for America. With its aerodynamic appearance, the Airstream's sleek silver monocoque body was designed to move through the air like a bullet. It remains a timeless icon of mobility. Twenty-five years later the Clark Cortez Camper, predecessor to the recreational vehicle (RV), combined the hitched-on trailer with the engine. This new hybrid package provided all the domestic comforts of home within reach of the steering wheel.

The Great Depression followed by the war effort required people to move where they could find work, and the demand for instant or emergency housing was heightened. During these years, over 200,000 trailers were mass-produced, with more than 60 percent of them located in defense-production areas. Following the war and the passage of the GI bill, colleges and universities responded to the influx of soldiers returning from the war, and the corresponding increase of married students, by introducing the trailer to campuses.

Concurrently, itinerant farm laborers and migrant factory workers in the early twentieth century were producing new examples of homemade house-cars and wagon-train caravans. These structures, born out of economic necessity, were later invoked in the movies, housing characters from the traveling evangelist/miracle healer to the circus/entertainer, in such films as Arthur Penn's 1970 *Little Big Man* and Federico Fellini's 1954 *La Strada*. These films depict a nostalgic yet realistic portrait of the nomad hustler who lives in places for brief moments, constructing the novelty of the spectacle, before rolling on.

## TRUCKS, TRAILER CULTURE, AND MANUFACTURED HOUSING

Beginning in the late 1930s and dominating the postwar years, mobile enterprise expanded to include "delivering, collecting, hauling, distributing, as well as making repairs." With the introduction of the transit shed and soon after the highway, the loading dock became an integral part of building design, and the tractor-trailer truck evolved. Replacing small immobile businesses, the truck enticed the mobile entrepreneur, giving rise to a new industrialized landscape. Social interaction had moved onto the strip, incorporating the drive-in—franchise restaurants, banks, liquor stores, package stores, car washes, dry cleaners, libraries—as permanent fixtures in the landscape.

With the advent of trucking, and in response to the postwar housing shortage, new mobile housing strategies developed, including the "flat-pack." Carl Koch (with Hudson Jack and John Callender) designed the Acorn House in 1945. Designed specifically with truck transportation in mind, this narrow unit, constructed of thirty-seven factory-made and -assembled component parts, had folding panels that opened to form living space and refolded for transport. Delivered to a site in a collapsed form, their condensed size made them advantageous for long-distance delivery and efficient when size, weight, and volume were restricted.

The flat-pack strategy lives on. In 1991, the now defunct magazine *Progressive Architecture* sponsored a competition to increase the quality of affordable housing and turned to the industrialized housing sector. (Referred to in the building industry as manufactured housing, 97 percent of these dwellings move only once, from the factory to a new trailer "park," where they remain permanently sited. Typically the building material is a lightweight, wooden superstructure on its own chassis with a permanently fixed set of wheels for easy transport.) The challenge of the *Progressive Architecture* competition was to design and build a single-family home for under $65,000. The winning scheme, by Abacus Architects in Boston, modified the assembly-line unit by combining the standard module and chassis with the flat-pack, a hinged collapsible roof that would lie flat in transit and unfold to form a conventional pitched roof on site. Fabricated in less than a month, the modules were erected in one day. With an emphasis on contextuality, the shotgun-style house was designed to slip unassumingly into a preexisting neighborhood.

The Abacus design addressed not only issues of efficiency and affordability but also initiated a serious aesthetic critique of trailers. As articulated by J. B. Jackson, "The Trailer has no real attachment to place." Its anonymity, disregard for regional contextualism, and inability to work with the contours of the natural landscape force the mobile dwelling to remain on the periphery of environmental design discourse, making the argument for its acceptance arduous.

Big rigs parked at a truck stop outside Charlotte, North Carolina.

The specificity of the material palette is essential to the body of work represented. Historically, people moved whole villages and hamlets when soil was exhausted or there was threat of an enemy attack. As J. B. Jackson points out in "The Movable Dwelling and How It Came to America," "For all their squalor medieval peasant dwellings had a remarkable flexibility and mobility—not only in that they could be taken down and reassembled elsewhere, but in that they could easily change function and change tenants....The temporary nature of the dwelling, its negligible material value, meant that it could be lightheartedly abandoned when crops failed, when war threatened, or when the local lord proved too demanding."[11]

Materials spoke of what was considered to be mobile and immobile, where the flimsiness of the construction protected the family from the dangers of staying put. The use of wood was a language of impermanence, while the use of stone was a symbol of solidity or immovability. Wood, a modest and abundant material, could be separated from the operation of the farm or detached and rapidly reassembled elsewhere. This was preferred over stone, which had lasting endurance but was not suitable for transport.

The American pioneers had a readily and seemingly unlimited material palette at their disposal. Wood was abundant and could be easily manipulated to provide material for simple structures that could be erected with minimal labor and in a relatively short time. The development of the box house emerged, constructed from single planks of wood nailed together vertically with no internal framing. The proliferation of these buildings was evident. Used as slave quarters on plantations and in mobile lumber towns and camps, they were inexpensive and easily relocatable by railroad, and later by automobile. In 1895 Sears and Roebuck offered enticing visual images creating a market for the ready-cut or mail-order house. As J. B. Jackson noted, "The real novelty was that these dwellings were built, occupied, and eventually disposed of as *commodities*, merchandise designed and produced to satisfy a definite market."[12]

Mass-produced housing started with John Manning, a London carpenter and builder who in 1830 designed the Manning Portable Colonial cottage. Designed to break down into component pieces that were then small enough to be stowed for shipping, "the Manning dwelling can be seen as the beginning of the prefabrication industry which produced products that utilized standardized interchangeable components and dimensional coordination to form easily erected flexible structures."[13] While the Manning cottage created new possibilities for the mobile-building industry, the monotony by which mass production evolved has incited such responses as Edgar Kaufmann Jr.'s: "Within the great impersonality of the world of mass production and new disposability there becomes clear for the first time the possibility of an intense personalism as a proper balance and as a proper enrichment of life. The future of design lies in situation design and not in product design; products merely implement the situations."[14]

A good example of situation design can be found in the collage of prefabricated parts in an ad-hoc settlement along Route 1 in Northern

Baja California. Mile marker seventy three indicates Campo Rivera, the site of unschooled, fanciful architecture. Similar to the conventional trailer park, each Campo Rivera compound stakes out a plot with an Airstream trailer as the keystone. This central wagon gives rise to a train of disparate parts: the addition, the outhouse, and the water tank, synthesized through an ingenious and adaptive use/reuse of materials. Inventiveness is shown in the manipulation of the modules, while individual identity is maintained by using a limited palette of components and materials.

All construction projects, even those designed for monumental permanence, make use of a palette of temporary materials. New freeways, bridges, and buildings of poured-in-place concrete rely uniformly on plywood formwork that is used until the material fails or is no longer valued in its present (scarred and unsightly) state. Increasingly, scaffolding is the most common form of temporary works used in the construction industry, because this modular system is easy to expand and demount. The use of scaffolding as a simple assembly procedure was used most notably by Tadao Ando, who de-signed the Karaza Theater, built in fifteen days in 1987. Renowned for his permanent buildings constructed with the use of pure concrete slabs, Ando designed the theater to be portable, with a vast majority of its structural elements made from locally sourced standard components. Additionally, one of the most well-known portable buildings is the Teatro del Mondo designed by Aldo Rossi for the Venice Biennale in 1979. Based on sixteenth-century floating pavilions, this temporary structure was built from steel scaffolding sheathed in wood and supported underneath by a large steel barge.

Through the 1960s, radical experiments by the U.K. collective Archigram (short for "architectural telegram") were stirring up imaginations and sowing the seeds for future uprisings. Growing out of the student discontent and the indeterminacy at the end of the 1950s, protest design magazines such as *Polygon*, *Clip-Kit*, *Megascope*, and *Archigram* gave voice to social commentators and urban agitators. Members of Archigram's inner circle developed ideas leading to Peter Cook's Plug-in City, Dennis

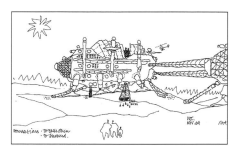

Early sketch for Walking City, 1964, by Ron Herron of Archigram.

Crompton's Computer City, and Ron Herron's Walking City. With its multifunctioning and infinitely reprogrammable body, detachable auxiliary units, and telescopic legs (which connected with other walking elements and with the ground and sea, allowing the transfer of goods and materials), Walking City was likened by the *International Times* to a war machine. Nomadism was a reoccurring theme, even way of life, among members in the Archigram group: They attended huge outdoor rock concerts like Woodstock and the Rolling Stones show in Hyde Park; they traveled the lecture circuit, performing as the Archigram Opera and touring the U.K. like a circus.

In 1970, these agitprop themes grew into Instant City, an exploration in indeterminacy of

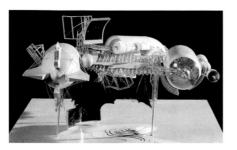

place, where the city is recognized as a changing entity capable of responding to the inhabitants' immediate needs. As Ron Herron noted, "The design for Instant City brought together trailer units, inflatables, lightweight structures, gantries, towers, support systems, scaffolding, audio-visual displays, projection equipment, and electronic display systems. The metropolis would arrive like the circus, set up shop, operate for a period of time, and then move on."

These "up-to-the-minute environments" (a phrase coined by Reyner Banham) were developing among contemporaries around the globe. Missing Link Productions in Vienna designed Fleder-Housing, a disposable housing unit for people with limited funds, and Golden Viennese Heart, a strategic multiuse mobile structure designed to allow people to interact directly with the forces that govern them (that is, a city hall for community confrontation). Cedirc Price's Phun City was a sixty-acre, self-help festival held in the Sussex countryside in 1970. The spontaneity of the experience was at the core of its success.

Such explosions of pop-up festival cities occur to this day. Notoriously, Burning Man Project draws thousands of revelers to the Black Rock Desert in northwestern Nevada every Labor Day weekend. These pilgrims bring with them the entire infrastructure for a small city located upon an alkali playa, where they erect a giant human figure that is ritualistically burned at the festival's close. Three days are devoted to ritual, art, and celebration. Participants see it as one of the last places on Earth where people from all walks of life, all social strata, and all points of the compass can come together and share a common and primal experience, surviving as a group in a challenging environment, creating a temporary culture of their own design, and sharing one of the most elemental experiences of our species—the mystery of fire.

Representing the end product of architectural ideologies promoting emancipation through industrialization, the inflatable environment, with its optimistic form and fragile monumentality, has provided radical architects with a new platform. As Mark Fisher recounts, the students of pneumatic design in England and France initially drew inspiration from Frei Otto's 1957–60 work, particularly his soap-bubble experiments and water-filled cylindrical membranes. The British engineer Frederick William Lanchester patented the first pneumatic structure in 1917, and Walter W. Bird initiated the American development called "radomes" in 1955 ; the students of the sixties embarked upon their own theoretical and built versions of these earlier ideas.

By the 1967 Paris Biennial, Jean Aubert, Jean-Paul Jungmann, and Antoine Stinco debuted Pneumatic Living-Economical-Mobile. In 1968, their group Utopie (whose thinking and name, like the Situationists, derives from Henri Lefebvre), were completing their end-of-studies diploma project at the École des Beaux-Arts when they found themselves exhausted by the industrial myth and constraint of pre-fabrication of building elements. Making real the theories of Lefebvre—"the need for play, spontaneity, the realization of desires and calls, the desire to rescue utopian imagination from science fiction, to invest all of technology into daily life," and to bring about "daring gestures" and "structures of enchantment"—they began research into pneumatic structures. "Allowing for a greater degree of spiritualization of the machine long sought by the avant-garde, a sort of communion in aerophagia between surrealism and the functionalist philosophy of doing the most with the least, inflatables would figure as the lightweight and elating supplement to the group's theoretical oeuvre." Their belief was that, "Unlike conventional architecture, which stands rigidly to attention and deteriorates (like a guardsman with moths in the busby), inflatables (and tents, to a lesser extent) move and are so nearly living and breathing that it is no surprise that they have to be fed (with amps, if not oats). All architecture has to mediate between an outer and an inner environment in some way, but if you can sense a rigid structure actually doing it

(dripping sounds, tiles flying off, windows rattling), it usually means a malfunction. An inflatable, on the other hand, in its state of active homeostasis, trimming, adjusting, and taking up strains, is malfunctioning if it doesn't squirm and creak. As an adjustable and largely self-regulating membrane it is more truly like the skin of a living creature than the metaphorical 'skin' of, say, a glass-walled office block."

The blue-sky, blow-up group of Coop Himmelb(l)au established its name and its work around projects such as Cloud I and Astro-Balloon. The Pneumacosm of Hana-Rucker-Co was a means of inducing continuing, open-ended process into existing cityscapes through the use of pneumatic dwelling units in vertical urban structures. Ant Farm in Sausalito, California, the self-proclaimed "truckin'-down-the-highway freaks" of the seventies, compiled the INFLATOCOOKBOOK, a collection of recipes for inflatoenvironments such as Truckin' University, a self-help truckable environment for turning on friends and faraway people; and Environmints, offering several flavors of inflatable polyethylene structures for gathering.

Antonio Sant'Elia proclaimed in 1914, "We no longer believe in the monumental, the heavy and static, and have enriched our sensibilities with a taste for lightness, transience, and practicality. We must invent and remake the Futurist city like an immense assembly yard, dynamic in every part; the Futurist house like a giant machine." Part of the "generation of electricity," Sant'Elia's drawings of the Città Futurista (1913–15) and the sketches for Power-Stations (1914) suggest an architecture of "diagonal and elliptical lines" and a firm belief that "architecture such as this breeds no permanence, [and] no structural habits." This leads us to Sant'Elia's conclusion

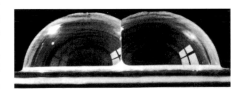

Burning Man Festival, 2000, Black Rock City, Nevada.

Frei Otto's tensile-stress pneumatic structures were developed through incessant experiments with soap-bubble models.

that "we shall live longer than our houses, and every generation will have to make its own city."[20]

Throughout the late twentieth century and into the twenty first, visionary architects have responded to Sant'Elia's Futurist claims. Paolo Soleri began his utopian vision in the Arizona desert and embarked on his journey of making his own city with the creation of Arcosanti in 1970. Designing according to the concept of arcology (architecture + ecology), Soleri stated that "Shifting Populations [will be] the norm in the future: The human species is on the move. When Asia and Africa follow suit, even at the exclusion of forcible shifts (political, economical, cultural, and racial), millions of people will expect shelter and services in the most likely and unlikely places. A prelude to the plunge into space, and Hilton Hotels are not where the answers will be."[21]

Another visionary, Rem Koolhaas, reshuffles our notions of the city and permanence, writing, "The Generic City is always founded by people on the move, poised to move on. This explains the insubstantiality of their foundations. Like the flakes that are suddenly formed in a clear liquid by joining two chemical substances, eventually to accumulate in an uncertain heap on the bottom, the collision or confluence of two migrations—Cuban émigrés going north and Jewish retirees going south, for instance, both ultimately on their way someplace else—establishes, out of the blue, a settlement."[22]

In his 1995 book *Visionary Architecture*, German author Christian W. Thomsen pointed to the future of cities in which buildings with adjustable, skin-like sensors detect motion, weight, and heat; cameras scan like eyes, microphones and speakers hear and talk, and alarms mimic fight-or-flight reactions, with the structures learning all the while by recording this information.[23]

Our current culture produces a wide variety of portable, relocatable, and demountable building types ranging from health-care to educational and commercial facilities. The portable culture has roving access to blood-donor and dental check-up stations, to book-mobiles, banks, food, and sanitary facilities. Through mobile deployment of these facilities the infrastructure is limitlessly expanded.

But portable and mobile architecture is not merely product design or a continued modification of the Conestoga or the Airstream. Rather it is a recognition of the fluidity of circumstances—the mobility of demographics and information—and an increasing capacity for architecture to respond to fluidity, whether through low-tech, ad hoc vernaculars or through

"Itinerant Exhibition Hall for Objects of Everyday Life," designed by Antoine Stinco, June 1967. A hybrid structure of four pneumatical spheres retained by a prestressed membrane.

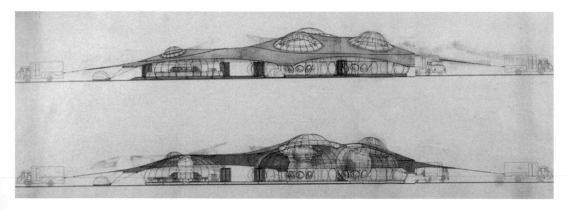

high-tech kinetics and embedded computation. These dwellings offer an alternative and possibly a solution for the inhabitants of the new "generic" landscape.

Douglas Heingartner, "Mobile Homer," *Artbyte* 3, no. 6 (April 2001): p. 62.

Guy Debord, *Society of the Spectacle* (Detroit, MI: Black & Red, 1983), section 42.

Robert Kronenburg, *Houses in Motion: The Genesis, History and Development of the Portable Building* (London: Academy Editions, 1995), p. 11.

Gilbert Herbert, *The Dream of the Factory-Made House* (Cambridge, MA: MIT Press, 1984), p. 106.

Kronenburg, *Houses in Motion*, p. 60.

Le Corbusier, *L'Esprit Nouveau*, No. 2, p. 211. As quoted in Kronenburg, *Houses in Motion*, p. 63, and Reyner Banham, *Theory and Design in the First Machine Age* (London: Architectural Press, 1960), p. 221.

Peter Sultzer, *Jean Prouvé: Complete Works, Volume 2: 1934–1944* (Basel: Birkhauser, 2000), p. 259.

Heingartner, "Mobile Homer," p. 63.

John Brinckerhoff Jackson, "The Movable Dwelling and How It Came to America," in *Discovering the Vernacular Landscape* (New Haven, CT: Yale University Press, 1984), p. 184.

Ibid., p. 60.

Ibid., p. 95.

Ibid., p. 96.

Kronenburg, *Houses in Motion*, p. 38.

Quoted in Ibid., p. 67.

"The Alchemy of the Ad Hoc," *The Los Angeles Forum for Architecture and Urban Design*, May 1995.

Quoted in Reyner Banham, *The Visions of Ron Herron* (London: Academy Editions, 1994), p. 45.

Frei Otto, *Tensile Structures* (Cambridge: MIT Press, 1967).

Marc Dessauce, ed., *The Inflatable Moment: Pneumatics and Protest in '68* (New York: Princeton Architectural Press and The Architectural League of New York, 1999), pp. 21, 33.

Quoted in Reyner Banham, *Design by Choice* (London: Academy Editions, 1981), p. 24.

Ibid., p. 24–25.

Soleri, Paolo, *ARCOSANTI: An Urban Laboratory?* (San Diego: Avant Books 1983), p. 26.

Rem Koolhaas, "Generic City," lecture transcript, Sikkens Foundation, Sassenheim, November 1995, p. 11.

Christian W. Thomsen, *Visionary Architecture: From Babylon to Virtual Reality* (New York: Prestel Publishers, 1994), pp. 172–173.

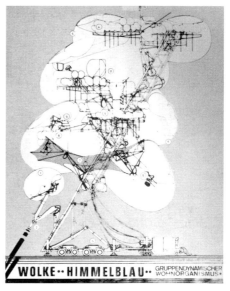

Cloud I, designed by Coop Himmelb(l)au for the Future Forms of Living program, 1968, is a set of individual inflatable pods clustered around a large communal pneumatic area, programmed for T-groups, sensitivity, and encounter sessions.

Sant'Elia's 1913 sketch for a power station anticipates contemporary engineering geometries.

IMAGE CREDITS

page 017: Torsten Schmiedeknecht, "The Ephemeral in the Work of Haus-Rucker-Co," *Architectural Design* 68 (Sept./Oct. 1998): p. 38.

page 019: Peter Sulzer, *Jean Prouvé: Complete Works, Vol. 2: 1934–44* (Basel: Birkhauser, 2000), p. 260.

page 020 top: *Trailer Life* (November 1967): cover.

page 020 bottom: Reyner Banham, *Design by Choice* (London: Academy Editions, 1981), p. 114.

page 021: Collection Office of Mobile Design.

page 023: Reyner Banham, *The Visions of Ron Herron* (London: Academy Editions, 1994), p. 16.

page 024: Reyner Banham, *The Visions of Ron Herron* (London: Academy Editions, 1994), p. 43.

page 025 top: Sean Christopher.

page 025 bottom: Frei Otto, *Tensile Structures* (Cambridge, MA: MIT Press, 1967), p. 13.

page 026: Marc Dessauce, ed., *The Inflatable Moment: Pneumatics and Protest in '68* (New York: Princeton Architectural Press and The Architectural League of New York, 1999), pp. 96–9.

page 027 left: Jim Burns, *Anthropods: New Design Futures* (New York: Praeger Publishers, 1971), p. 103.

page 027 right: Reyner Banham, *Design by Choice* (London: Academy Editions, 1981), p. 27.

page 029: Jonathan Bell, *Carchitecture* (Basel: Birkhauser, 2001), p. 33.

The installation U-town, 1998, by artist Steven Brower, is a vision of Buckminster Fuller-esque American trailer-park culture, uniting the geodesic dome with the 1933 (pre-SUV) tri-wheeled Dymaxion Car.

# FESTO

Professor Axel Thallemer, founder of Festo Corporate Design, was born in 1959 in Munich-Schwabing. He studied science theory, logic, and theoretical linguistics at the Ludwig-Maximilians University, Munich, and received a degree in civil engineering at the Academy of Fine Arts, Munich. He received a postgraduate scholarship to study business, public relations, and psychology at the New York School of Interior Design, and currently teaches computer-aided design as well as corporate design at the Munich University of Applied Sciences. In 1994 Thallemer founded Festo and, through strategic development, spearheaded Festo's transition from a subconsciously lived brand family to a truly global master brand enabling holistic, multidisciplinary approaches. Thallemer is a member of the International Council of Societies of Industrial Design, the German Design Council, and the Industrial Designers Society of America. He has lectured and published widely.

Thallemer's works of design are included in the permanent collections of several international museums. His Fluidic Muscle project has received several awards, including the Good Design Award from the Japanese Ministry of International Trade and Industry (1998), the Best of Category/Industry–Product Design Award from the Industry Forum Hanover (1999), the Red Dot Highest Design Quality Award from the Design Center North Rhine Westphalia (1999), the Techtextil Innovation Prize from the Scientific Advisory Board of the International Techtextil Symposium (1999), and the Federal Award for Product Design from the Federal Ministry for Economics and Technology (2000). In 2001 Festo was heralded as Design Team of the Year by Design Center North Rhine Westphalia.

In 2002 Thallemer was appointed Fellow of the Royal Society of the Arts, London, U.K.

# AIRTECTURE

The first building in the world to be constructed with a cubic interior (comprised of supporting structures built with air-inflated chambers) has been unveiled by Festo in the form of an exhibition hall. Festo firmly believes that the innovative ideas behind this structure, developed in the Pneumatic Structures Group, (recently established by the Department of Civil engineering at the University of Newcastle upon Tyne) and the new applications for which it can be used are excellent prerequisites for setting new trends in the world of construction engineering.

The inside of the hall is 6 meters tall with a floor area of 375 square meters and has a total volume of 2,250 cubic meters. The exterior dimensions of the hall are a ground area of 800 square meters with a height of 7.2 meters. The structure is relatively light, having a dead load of 7.5 kg/square meters. The air-inflated chambers of the exhibition hall are made with textile membranes, which can be folded up in a 40-foot container and transported to different locations quickly and efficiently, thanks to the low overall weight of 6 tons.

The load-bearing structure of the exhibition hall includes forty Y-shaped columns and thirty-six wall components along both longitudinal sides. Seventy-two thousand distance threads per square meter hold the double layer walls in place. The slits between the opaque wall components are filled with transparent cushions made of Hostaflon ET; these window sections can be easily replaced by means of slide locks. The load-bearing structure also features a double-wall fabric, flame-inhibiting elastomer coatings, and a new translucent ethylene-vinyl acetate coating.

Festo has been exploring new territories in the field of air-conditioning. In addition to natural ventilation through the two doors, conditioned air is distributed via two textile-supply air ducts,

suspended from the ceiling. Gravel filling under the grating is used as a heat-storage medium; light gravel from the Rhine river keeps infrared absorption to a minimum. Radiators in the air space between the grating and gravel bed ensure that the temperature in the hall remains constant during the winter. During the summer, a cooling system counteracts higher temperatures inside the hall.

AIRQUARIUM

As Festo investigated functionality in the air and through air, they created a new brand called "Air in Air." Within the Air in Air framework Festo realized another portable architectural idea in the area of pneumatics and thus innovated the classic inflatable structure. Whereas Airtecture is characterized by rectangular cross sections and parallel walls, Airquarium incorporates a spherical shell that provides an even greater amount of mobility.

A key feature of the project is the water-filled torus that serves as a foundation and also refers to our newly developed membrane material, which, supported by air, spherically expands over the foundation ring. To our knowledge, there is no other transparent/translucent textile membrane cupola in the world that combines such a great span with an extremely high level of translucency. Despite its size—thirty two meters in diameter and eight meters in height—the Airquarium can be stored in two 20-foot containers. One container holds all of the modular maintenance units, such as air conditioning, ventilation, water exchanger for cooling and heating, emergency generator for independent power supply for more than forty-eight hours of

operation, weather station, thermostat control, and wind-load-dependent air-pressure control. The second container holds the Vitroflex shell and the membrane foundation torus (of course, without the 120-ton water ballast) including the entrance tunnel and airlock.

New visions always require new materials and production processes for their realization, but we also place great value on sustainable design. Therefore, we have used a special type of caoutchouc for Airquarium that has been provided by Bayer; it exhibits a unique transparency and resistance to tearing. The Conti-Tech company has produced Vitroflex from this material, which is then manufactured into ready-to-use structures by Koch Membranes.

# COCOON

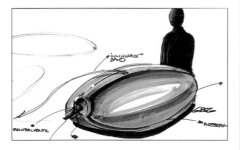

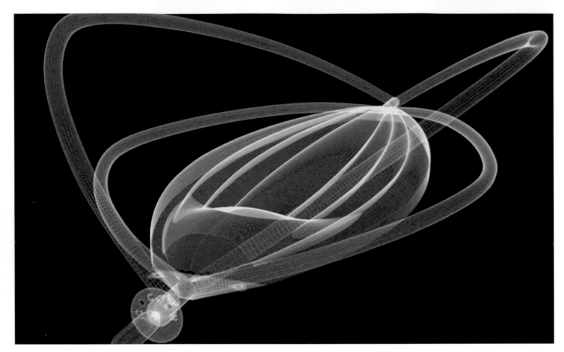

Cocoon is a small, light-weight, inflatable mini-tent. The tent can be inflated using a standard handpump or a supplied gas cartridge and can be erected quickly and easily by one person. This results in self-explanatory design and usage. The tent can be used not only for leisure activities such as sport and travel but also in rescue situations and disaster areas.

Similar to an insect's cocoon, the tent's design reflects new areas of application. Translucent airbeams allow daylight into the tent. If necessary, fluorescent tubes (safety lights) can be used to illuminate the interior of the tent at night. The outer shell is made of multilayer sheeting, which is particularly conspicuous due to its color. The sheeting reflects body heat back into the tent and, at the same time, repels low temperatures from the surrounding environment.

The tent is insulated against low-ground temperatures by its base sheet, which is designed as an inflatable mattress, and is extremely compact to ensure minimum transport volume with purpose-oriented design. Owing to its well-conceived basic structure and its single-part design, the tent can be manufactured in one single cycle. This provides ecological and economical benefits thanks to a single-piece production tool and small amount of waste cuttings from the base materials of the tent.

The product is highly mobile owing to its minimum transport volume and weight. Simple erection takes place in three steps: roll out the tent, inflate the pneumatic structure, fold up the airbeams. A roll of standard adhesive tape is supplied with the tent for repairs, making maintenance simple and quick.

A 100-micrometer thick polyurethane sheet is sufficient to give the tent a high degree of stability. Only the base has a more robust, fabric-reinforced sheet in order to prevent damage to the tent if erected on rough ground. There are no rigid rods to hold up the tent, as

this is taken care of by the inflated airbeams.

All in all, the amount of material used in the Cocoon is significantly less than that of conventional tents. The material is bonded by thermal impulse welding, and no adhesives are required. All of the materials were selected with recyclability and durability in mind for maximum efficiency with minimum material requirements.

# FLUIDIC MUSCLE

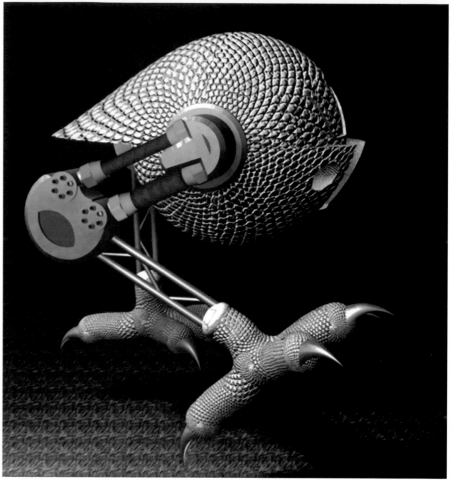

The fluidic muscle is a hose that consists of alternate layers of elastomer and fibers and can be operated as an actuator with compressible as well as noncompressible fluids.

By building up internal pressure using a fluid medium, the contraction hose shortens along its longitudinal axis. This shortening is directly proportional to the fill volume, enabling exact positioning without servo-control-electronics, using only the straightforward membrane regulator for the internal pressure. We call this "low-tech/low-cost positioning." By winding filaments in different ways, a three-dimensionally expanding helical net is formed. This textile reinforcement transfers the actual movement and force. As this actuator, unlike classic drives, has no piston or

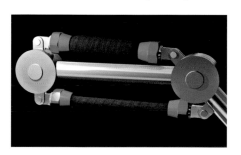

sealing ring (that is, no movable parts), this is the only drive that is stick-slip free. In traditional drive units there is static friction between the plunger gasket and the inner wall of the cylinder even when at rest. Only from a certain point of force does the so-called "breakaway moment" switch in, and then there follows the transition to sliding friction. The change from static to sliding friction is shown in a strong "jerking" of the drive, particularly at lower operating pressures. As Fluidic Muscle does not have this disadvantage, it can be operated gently and smoothly from standstill (without pressure) to maximum load.

The elastomer serves to seal off the operating fluid hermetically. The advantages compared to the traditional actuator are, among others, an initial force of up to ten times at the same nominal diameter, a fraction of its own weight, absolutely no stick-slip effect, and very simple positioning. The enormous agility of the Fluidic Muscle is shown in its superior behavior in acceleration and deceleration. The simplicity of the product allows the actuator to be cut with a normal pair of scissors when required and fixed in cone clamps, ready to

operate. There are no moving parts, and the membrane contraction system consists of only three different components. Each part can be exchanged or reconfigured by the user. Unlike other actuators, Fluidic Muscle needs no lubricants or coolants.

# BALLOONING

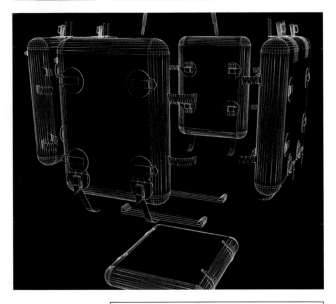

Ninety-two years after the first Gordon Bennett Coup Aéronautique, Festo unveiled a revolution in balloon racing: the world's first inflatable basket. Unlike traditional wicker baskets, which have remained unchanged for nearly two hundred years, the innovative pneumatic construction of this new basket represents a major advance in gas-balloon technology. Choice materials, novel ballast distribution, and integrated discharge paths for static electricity are the distinct advantages of the new Festo basket.

Pneumatic modules made of coated Conti-Tech fibers and inflated with compressed air make up the basket's supporting frame and provide clear advantages in terms of weight. A two-ply membrane covering the spaces between framework components allows pilots to carry up to 600 liters of water within the sides of the basket, thus eliminating much of the need to use sand bags for ballast. For safety reasons, ballast water is distributed among several chambers and can be drained either as needed or entirely, in the event of an emergency.

Gas balloons require increased safety precautions, especially when it comes to the necessity to discharge static electricity; for this reason Festo has integrated a network of conductive material into the basket's protective exterior. Achieving the necessary conductivity in wicker baskets has traditionally meant weaving copper wiring into the basket's structure. The conductivity of Festo's new basket material, however, along with its support cables, which connect to the exterior support rack at points beneath the basket floor, provide ten times the minimum specific resistance required for gas-balloon baskets by the German Civil Aviation Authority.

Gas-balloon races cover large distances and take place over the course of several days. For this reason Festo has equipped its basket with a solar sail and rain gear, plus a built-in berth so that pilots have a chance to rest. The basket also comes with the means of fastening down all equipment securely, including oxygen cylinders and electronic instruments, even during the roughest landings. The inflatable basket's excellent floatation properties also eliminate the need for the life rafts that would traditionally be used in emergency water landings.

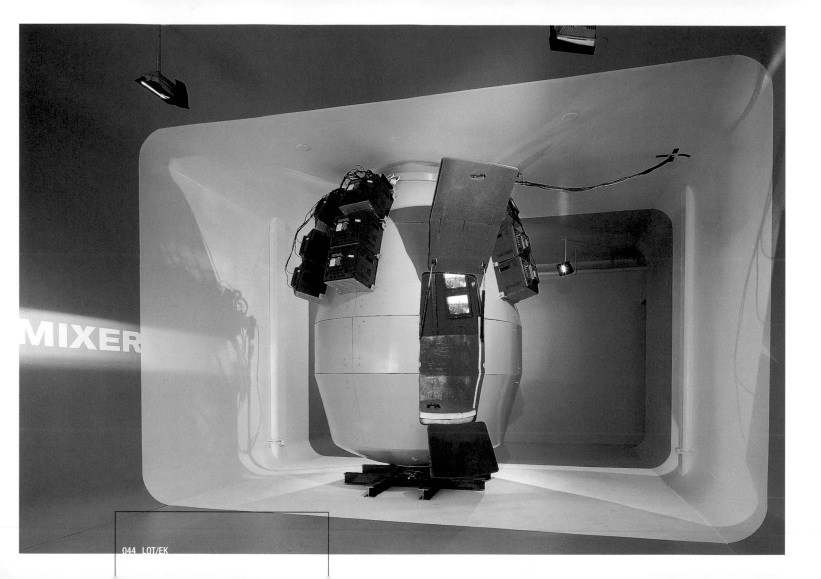

MIXER

# LOT/EK

LOT/EK is an architecture studio based in New York City. It was founded in 1993 by Ada Tolla and Giuseppe Lignano. Since then, LOT/EK has been involved in residential and commercial projects both in the Unites States and abroad, as well as exhibition design and site-specific installations for major cultural institutions and museums, including New York's Museum of Modern Art, Whitney Museum of American Art, Solomon R. Guggenheim Museum, and New Museum.

Ada Tolla and Giuseppe Lignano both earned master degrees in architecture and urban design from the University of Napoli, Italy (1989), and completed postgraduate studies at Columbia University, New York (1990–91). Besides heading their professional practice, they currently teach at Parsons School of Design, Graduate School of Architecture, in New York. They also lecture at major universities and cultural institutions throughout the world, including Columbia University, Yale University, Rice University, Rhode Island School of Design, the Museum of Modern Art, the Guggenheim Museum, Eidgenössische Technische Hochschule (Zurich); Escola Técnica Suprior d'Arquitectura de Barcelona; Istituto Universitario di Architettura di Venezia (Venice); and Bartlett and Royal College of Art (London).

The office has achieved high visibility in the architecture/design/art world for its innovative approach to construction, materials, and space, and for the use of technology as an integral part of architecture. Its projects are published in national and international publications, magazines, and books such as the *New York Times Magazine*, *Wall Paper*, *Domus*, *A+U*, *Interior Design*, *Wired*, *Surface*, *Metropolis*, *Vogue*, and *Harper's Bazaar*. Princeton Architectural Press released a monograph on LOT/EK in 2002.

# MIXER/
# MEDIA COCOON

Mixer transforms a steel cement-mixer into a twenty-first-century media cocoon suitable for lounging, viewing, and dreaming. Fitted with twelve-inch monitors connected to a variety of audiovisual inputs (surveillance cameras, satellite TV, DVD player, PlayStation 2), Mixer offers a plush, intimate environment animated by multiple forms of information and media. As

Mixer pivots on its central axis, Surveillance Camera #1 surveys the room in which the Mixer is located. Cables, coming out of the upper slip-ring, reach the roof of the building to connect to Satellite TV and to Surveillance Camera #2. City landscapes are transmitted to the monitors inside the Mixer together with the infinite channel selection of Satellite TV. Play-Station 2 brings virtual reality games, movies, and fast Internet connection into this capsule. Resting on extrasoft blue foam, users can create multiple visual configurations on twelve screens through a central router for a media overload. Mixer offers, in the spirit of a DJ mixing booth, a space for one or more people to select, sample, and mix sound and imagery to suit individual fantasies.

The Ret.Inevitable projection room is defined by stretching white spandex floor to ceiling. Visual programs are rear-projected onto the dynamic illuminated walls employing large mirrors to double the image size. Red navigation lights direct people to the entrance, where four slits allow entry to the core. Once inside, video art and short films engulf the viewers in a 360-degree experience. Blue vinyl-coated pool lounge chairs are mounted directly on the floor on a turntable mechanism to allow viewers to spin around. Each chair is equipped with infrared remote headsets that control sound and program selection. Ret.Inevitable1.5 investigates the experience of viewing cinema per se, exploring the physical aspect of total absorption in a cinematographic space.

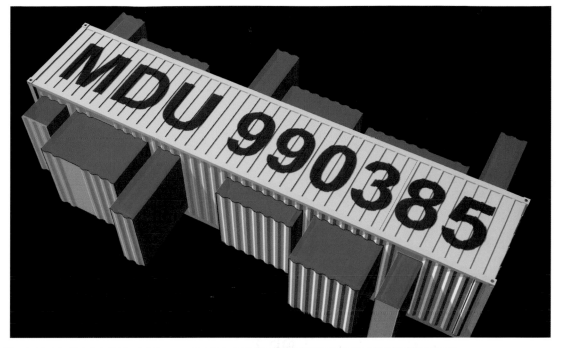

# MDU (Mobile Dwelling Unit)

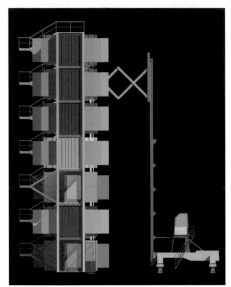

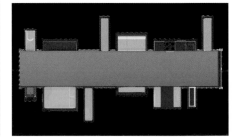

One shipping container is transformed into a Mobile Dwelling Unit. Cuts in the metal walls of the container generate extruded subvolumes, each encapsulating a single live, work, or storage function. When traveling, these subvolumes are pushed in, filling the entire container, interlocking with each other, and leaving the outer skin of the container flush to allow worldwide standardized shipping. When in use, all subvolumes are pushed out, leaving the interior of the container completely unobstructed with all functions accessible along its sides. The interior of the container and the subvolumes—including all fixtures and furnishings—are fabricated entirely out of fiberglass. A central computer regulates airflow and temperature as well as lighting, and is connected with all communication networks, monitors, and speakers/microphones throughout the unit. MDUs are conceived for individuals moving around the globe.

The MDU travels with its dweller to the next long-term destination, fitted with all live/work equipment and filled with the dweller's belongings. Once it reaches its destination, the MDU is loaded into MDU vertical harbors located in all major metropolitan areas around the globe. The harbor is a multiple-level steel rack, measuring 8 feet in width (the width of one container) and varying in length according to the site. Its stretched linear development is generated by the repetition of MDUs and vertical distribution corridors. Elevators, stairs, and all systems (power, data, water, sewage) run vertically along these corridors. A crane slides parallel to the building, along the entire length, on its own tracks. It picks up MDUs as they are driven to the site and loads them onto slots along the rack. Steel brackets support and secure MDUs in their assigned position, where they are plugged-in to connect to all systems. The vertical harbor is in constant transformation as MDUs

are loaded and unloaded from the permanent rack. Like pixels in a digital image, temporary patterns are generated by the presence or absence of MDUs in different locations along the rack, reflecting the ever-changing composition of these colonies scattered around the globe.

052  FTL HAPPOLD

# FTL HAPPOLD

FTL Happold is a design and engineering services firm with an emphasis on lightweight and deployable constructions, prefabricated structures, and flexible interiors. FTL Happold's design approach merges lighting, form, structure, environment, and acoustics to create complex three-dimensional surfaces and spaces. The firm uses special physical fabric modeling techniques and proprietary computer software for form generation, analysis, patterning, and graphics.

The formal union of FTL and Buro Happold began after a twenty-year collaboration and a five-year partnership. The long-range goal of the combined firm is the integration of architecture, engineering, and environmental design into a unified discipline of building design.

Principal Todd Dalland, FAIA, graduated from Cornell University with a Bachelor of Architecture degree. He began his career in 1971, designing and building tensile structures. Dalland founded FTL in 1977 and, over the past twenty five years, has been principal-in-charge of numerous projects, including the Pier 6 Concert Pavilion in Baltimore and the AT&T Global Olympic Village in Atlanta. Principal Nicholas S. Goldsmith, FAIA, graduated from Cornell University with a Bachelor of Architecture degree. He worked with Frei Otto in Stuttgart, Germany, and joined FTL as a principal in 1978. Goldsmith has been principal-in-charge of projects such as the Metropolitan Opera Travelling Facility and the DKNY World Headquarters.

# CARLOS MOSELEY MUSIC PAVILION

The Carlos Moseley Music Pavilion is a state-of-the-art performance facility designed for the Metropolitan Opera, the New York Philharmonic, and the City of New York's Departments of Cultural Affairs and Parks and Recreation for audiences of up to one hundred thousand people.

Completely mobile, six custom semitrailers carry the entire facility to any open performance site. Designed to be set up in three hours with minimal impact on fragile park locations, this traveling music pavilion has no precedent. The pavilion's pyramidal open-truss structure incorporates a translucent fabric shell, 40-by-78-foot folding stage, computerized lighting system, video projection screen, and a distributed sound system employing twenty-four wireless remote speaker towers.

Originally we worked on a series of schemes using a pyramid-frame structure consisting of four hydraulic cranes that docked in space. No manufacturer would allow standard cranes, so instead we used three 86-foot-long custom truss masts. We came up with an underfold apparatus on the front two trailers and a double-back device on the rear trailer. From this arrangement, the design took shape. Six semitrailers plus three dressing-room trucks transport the complete facility from park to park. These trailers hold all equipment necessary for setting up and dismantling the pavilion, including forklifts, hydraulic opening devices, and winches. The vehicles have been completely rebuilt to carry concrete foundations and meet all interstate highway regulations. In fact, the allowable weight of the trailers for highway travel ultimately determined the exact surface area of the overhead tensile fabric shell.

The basic design approach called for the fabric membrane to take its shape from the reflective acoustic requirements and the need to provide cover for the stage. The architectural poetry was found in the proportions and the relations of these elements to one another. The project then became a mixture of design, engineering, and mechanics, thereby raising the question: When is a structure a machine and when is it a building?

# AT&T GLOBAL
# OLYMPIC VILLAGE

Atlanta, and was designed to travel to future Olympic venues: Nagano in 1998, Sydney in 2000, and Salt Lake City in 2002. The structure's fabric was designed to be an entertainment effect in itself, allowing images from live Olympic events and live concerts to be projected 200 feet wide onto the outside of the building.

The village pavilions are demountable buildings that come close to the limit of feasibility. Two giant arched pavilions—the Media Pavilion and the Athletes Pavilion—created an exedral focus to Centennial Park. These were designed with steel truss arches, a PVC polyester membrane, glass and metal curtain walls, custom holographic walls, integrated lighting, and special furniture.

The Olympic Centennial Park's major facility was the AT&T Global Olympic Village, a $30 million, 9,000-square-foot complex comprising three relocatable buildings. The village incorporated two-story, relocatable glass curtain walls, relocatable interior elevators, and a second-story bridge between buildings. It debuted at the 1996 Summer Olympics in

The form of these pavilions is based on a series of Gothic truss arches that create a cathedral-like climax at a central performance stage. The fabric along the trusses is transparent and creates a clerestory colored with over 2,000 theatrical lights. A bit-mapped video system allows projection on the curved arch walls without distortion, creating a building as media icon.

This project required a central facility to showcase approximately sixty fashion shows during a seven-day New York "market week," which occurs every spring and fall, formerly held at designers' showrooms. The new central location would save time and help focus the energy and attention of the fashion buyers and the international news media that cover these high-profile events.

To meet these needs, FTL Happold designed a "tented fashion village" located in the newly restored Bryant Park adjacent to the New York Public Library. The complex consists of two large tented theaters, backstage tents, covered walkways, and a temporary infrastructure of power, heating, air conditioning, and toilets. Inside the village, the Josephine Pavilion accommodates 794 people and the Gertrude Pavilion accommodates 1,073. FTL Happold also designed the proscenium arches and runway "softlight," the fabric beacon tower at the corner of Forty-second Street and Sixth Avenue, as well as some stage sets, including several for Donna Karan. Set-up time for the entire complex requires less than six days.

# TIME FOR PEACE PAVILION

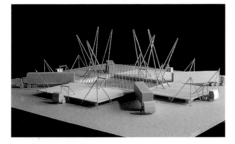

lation transforming the entire space into a painted environment. In the Information Chamber the visitor is taken on a didactic voyage through the history of conflict. In the Communication Chamber the visitor is immersed in an interactive media experience. In the Special Event Chamber diverse activities such as concerts, plays, and performances are held.

The Time for Peace Pavilion is a mobile architectural pavilion designed to travel throughout the world. Conceived by artists Robert and Marion Einbeck, this sculptural and streamlined project is aimed to raise the public consciousness of the possibilities of peace.

The Time for Peace Pavilion is a building on wheels that moves from site to site, carrying its own structure, enclosure, floors, interiors and infrastructure. This mobility gives the pavilion the flexibility to adapt to multiple uses at individual sites.

The interior of the pavilion is divided into five spaces dedicated to information, education, communication, and art. The centerpiece and largest of the five chambers, the Chamber of Reflection, contains an enormous art instal-

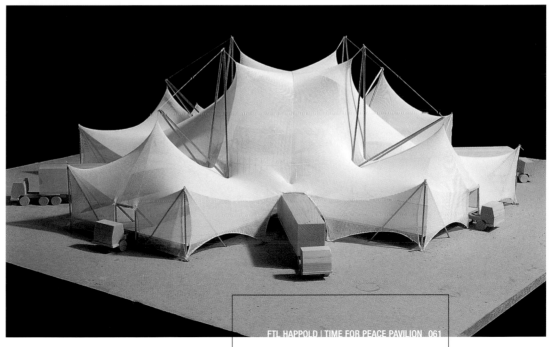

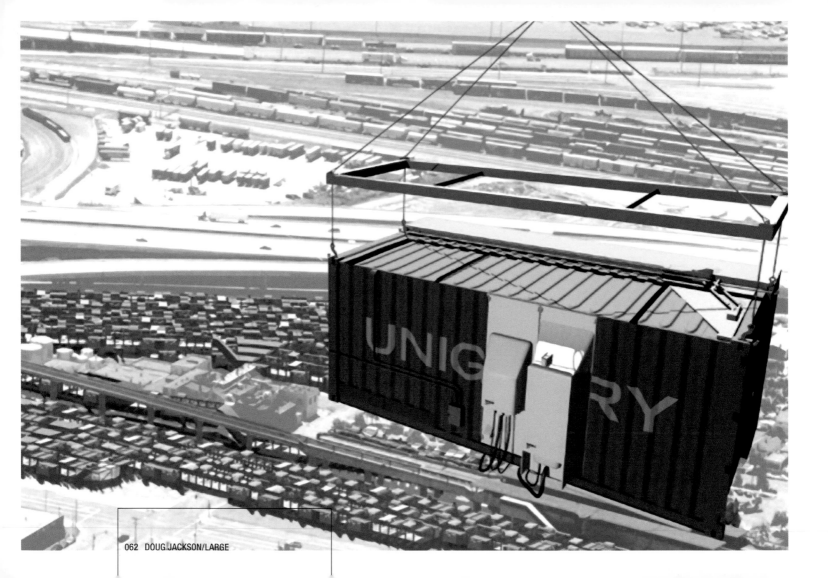

# DOUG JACKSON/LARGE

Doug Jackson was born in 1970 in Hampton, Virginia, and received his B.Arch. degree from Virginia Polytechnic Institute and his M.Arch. degree from Princeton University. From 1993 to 1998 he worked as a senior associate for Wes Jones at Jones, Partners: Architecture, where he served as the project architect on such works as the Confluence Point Bridge and Ranger Station in San Jose, California, and the Andersen Consulting Corporate Offices in Kuala Lumpur. He was also the graphic designer for Jones's award-winning monograph *Instrumental Form*. In 1999 he formed his own design-oriented practice, LARGE, in Los Angeles. LARGE pursues design across a broad spectrum, including architecture, furniture, and graphic design. The office's current projects include the Casa Vertical in Los Angeles, California, the Allington Residence in Phillips, Wisconsin, and the Diatomic Sofa.

# THE e-HIVE

To demonstrate the possibilities of a networked dwelling, we proposed a community of digitally and physically networked spaces known as the e-HIVE for a 22-acre site in the industrial port area of Oakland, California. Located immediately adjacent to the West Oakland BART (Bay Area Rapid Transit) station and just north of the Port of Oakland's Southern Pacific Railway Intermodal Yard, this particular site is characterized by empty expanses of asphalt and chain-link fence spread beneath the elevated portion of Oakland's I-880 freeway and punctuated occasionally by low, preengineered warehouse structures.

In order to maximize the flexibility of the e-HIVE system, its spatiality is redefined in terms of single individuals. The primary spatial

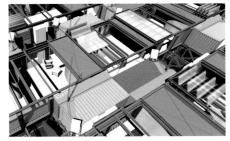

components of this system, therefore, are standardized and largely self-sufficient individual dwelling units.

Outfitted with autostereoscopic display screens—which accommodate the majority of the occupants' needs for aesthetic and recreational desires via telepresent connectivity, remote views, and interactive entertainment

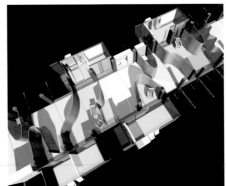

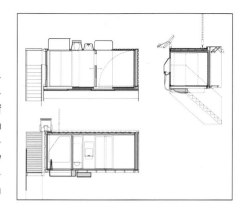

(the "software")—the individual dwelling units themselves are free to remain neutral and unadorned (the "hardware"). Based on a modified 20-foot ISO shipping container, the unit can accept various standardized "plug-in" fixture modules to accommodate storage or hygiene needs. A transverse sliding partition within the unit allows the occupant to create a physical separation between mediated and unmediated spaces, or between two different types of mediated spaces, as chosen. When daylight is desired during hours when it is not naturally available, daylight-temperature light fixtures mounted to the exterior collector can supply it. Thus, the individual unit is not shackled by the real time within which it is located, but rather can accommodate the idiosyncratic schedule of its occupant.

Although telepresence will allow for a wide range of social and spatial interactivity, and these types of mediated activities may ultimately come to largely supplant some of the face-to-face activities engaged in at present, they will likely never be universally seen as an adequate or desirable substitute. (Coined by Marvin Minsky in 1980, the term "telepresence"

refers to the use of any type of mediated communication technology with sufficient bandwidth to impart the sense among its users of being in the same environment with each other.) While this proposal anticipates a near-future when telepresence will be sufficiently facile to drive a reconceptualization of architectural space, it is not the only mechanism

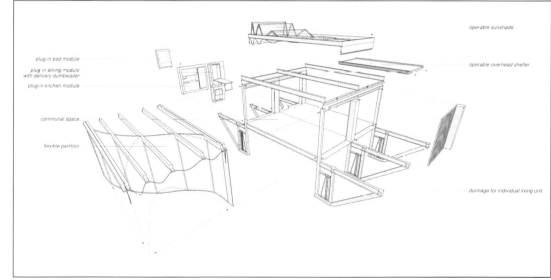

operable sunshade

operable overhead shelter

plug-in bed module

plug in dining module
with delivery dumbwaiter

plug-in kitchen module

communal space

flexible partition

dunnage for individual living unit

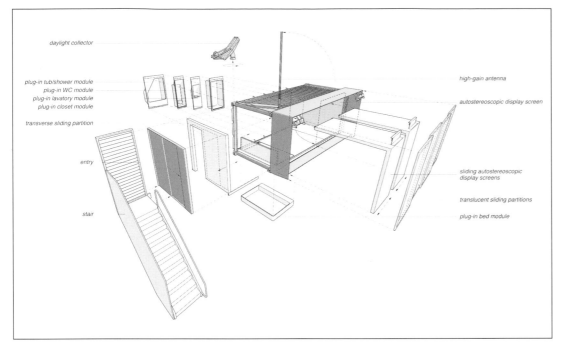

daylight collector

plug-in tub/shower module
plug-in WC module
plug-in lavatory module
plug-in closet module

transverse sliding partition

entry

stair

high-gain antenna

autostereoscopic display screen

sliding autostereoscopic
display screens

translucent sliding partitions

plug-in bed module

of connectivity provided for by this system. Rather than set such connectivity as the rule, however, this system proposes to allow it to be established on an ad hoc basis between neighboring units.

The e-HIVE is therefore comprised of a modular system of outdoor covered space into which the individual container units can be docked, as well as plug-in accessory units for kitchen, dining, conjugal activity, public entertainment, utility functions, and the like. Flexible silicon rubber partitions suspended from a two-degree-of-freedom carriage system, in conjunction with retractable translucent perimeter screens, allow for enclosed space to be created as desired, either interior or exterior, and either annexed to a single unit or conjoining multiple units. When a flexible partition is folded back on itself against a deployed perimeter screen, an enclosed outdoor storage space is created. Mobile furniture can be stowed within this enclosure when not needed and deployed when the flexible enclosure is opened up to make an inhabitable space.

This system assumes that these congregational spaces will be used on an event-specific basis. The architectural strategies appropriate to permanent space have therefore been traded away in favor of flexibility, and the system's surfaces remain relatively mute and purpose-driven. This aspect of the system derives its architectural interest directly from its variability: from its ability to weave together interior and exterior, and to extend and connect the individual dwelling units with a new type of space based upon a nonrectilinear formalism that arises directly from its need to be flexible. Furthermore, by enlisting the occupant as an agent of the physical networking of individual spaces, the e-HIVE gives, by analogy, palpable expression to the digital connectivity that it also provides.

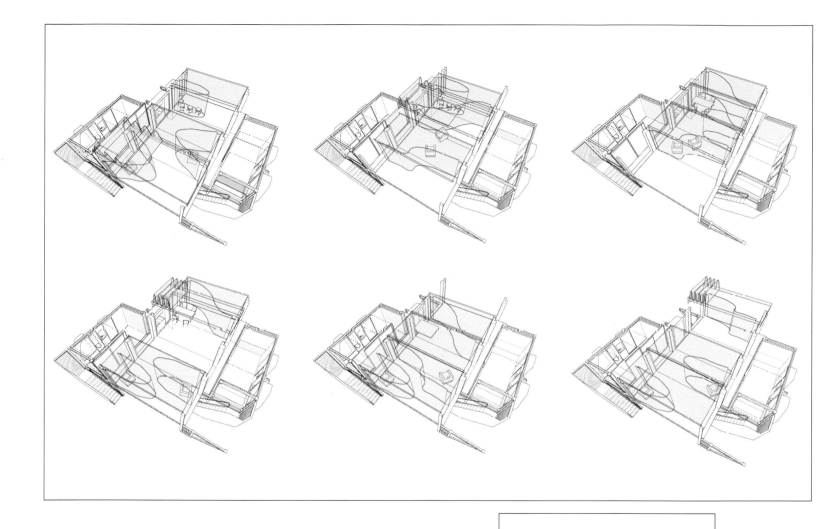

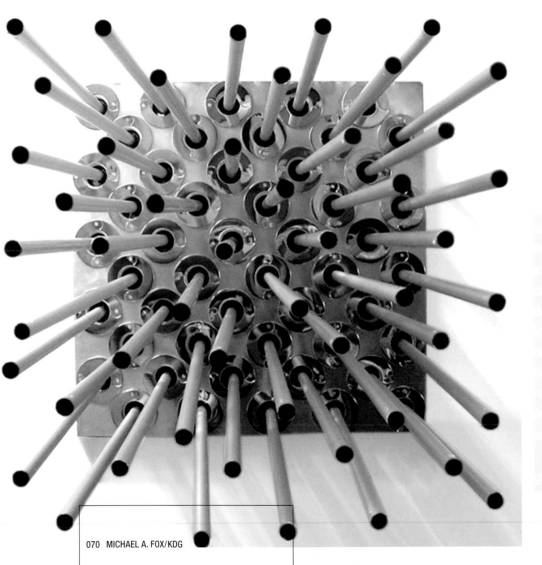

# MICHAEL A. FOX/KDG

systems at MIT, Fox has taught design studios at the Boston Architectural Center and a course on moderating behaviors in intelligent architecture at Hong Kong Polytechnic University. Fox received a professional degree in architecture from the University of Oregon in 1991 and a SMArchS in Design Technology from MIT in 1996.

Michael Fox has served as a personal assistant to engineer and inventor Chuck Hoberman in New York, working on the design and model construction of large-scale kinetic structures. As a design team leader for Kitamura Associates in Tokyo, Japan, he continued to explore kinetic functions as a design strategy for making spaces flexible, adaptive, and multi-usable. He has recently joined forces with Roark Associates to head a collaborative office in Los Angeles.

Fox has won numerous awards, including the Domus/BBJ Design Competition for New Ideas, the Kumamoto ArtPolis, and the Medina Intelligent Village Design Competition. Fox's work has been featured in various international publications including *Domus*, *LeMonde*, *Technology Review*, *Studio Voice*, and *Architecture*, and has been exhibited in the León Bienalle, Kumamoto ArtPolis, Milano Trienalle, and the Media Lab MindFest, and will be featured in an upcoming exhibit in the National Building Museum in Washington, D.C.

# INTERACTIVE KINETIC FACADE

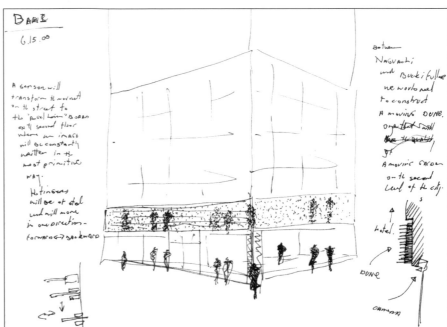

This project fosters direct interaction between an architectural-scale installation and pedestrian activity on the street. The 160-foot-long band of responsive "whiskers" that will wrap around a building in New York allows pedestrians to walk up to and interact with the installation. The bars move in wavelike rhythm driven by sensors, mounted beneath each row, that

monitor the presence of a moving person. If motion is detected, the poles gradually point toward the target, creating a ripple through the field. Each element moves in a simple fashion but together more complex patterns evolve. The project at once engages individual interactivity and at the same time actively mirrors unengaged pedestrian activity as a whole.

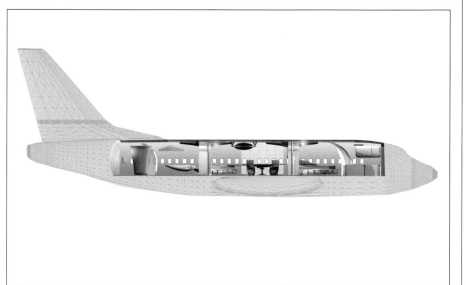

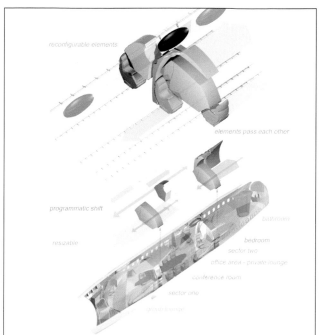

reconfigurable elements

elements pass each other

programmatic shift

resizable

bathroom

bedroom

sector two

office area - private lounge

conference room

sector one

group lounge

# BOEING BUSINESS JET INTERIOR

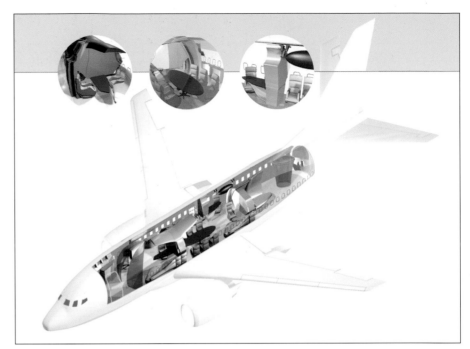

The motivation for this project was to create interior design solutions that are flexible and adaptive and, at instances, responsive and intelligently active with respect to changing individual, social, and climatic contexts. Accordingly, the goal was to provide a responsive interior space that can be configured as prescribed by the users prior to a specific flight as well as partially reconfigured in-flight. Such adaptability aims to meet the changing needs of the users and their activities/environment for comfort and optimum spatial efficiency. The design proposal introduces to the interior three basic kinetic components: sectors (which display variable location), mobility, and transformability (variable geometry). The sectors can technically operate independently; as a complete

system, they divide and define zones of the program in the interior. Each is equipped with or otherwise provides the technical and the physical/spatial apparatuses necessary for various parts of the program.

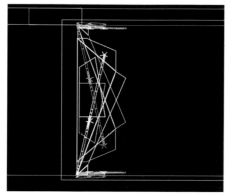 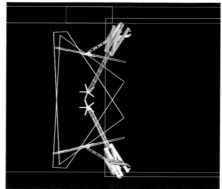

Eight automated doors, four on each floor, operate in a choreographed sequence for an automobile lift. Servo-controlled cylinders direct the motion without the use of rails or cables. An automobile collection is housed and displayed in the building with the elevator connecting several floors and serving as the central piecc dividing the spaces. Aluminum framing, stainless steel cylinders, and a stainless steel mesh wall combine to make this composed mechanism. The doors can be programmed to open in a number of ways to create dynamic and changing entry sequences for the client.

With Roart Inc., New York.

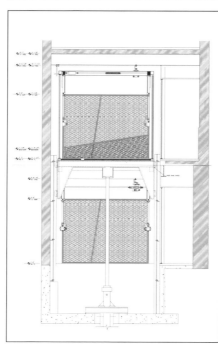

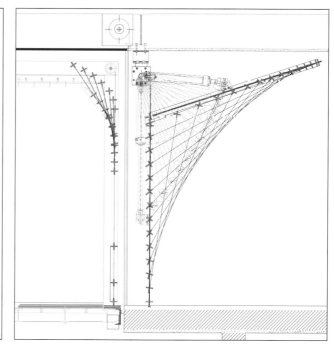

# RESPONSIVE SKYLIGHTS

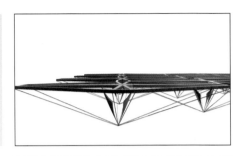

The Responsive Skylights is a networked system of individually responsive skylights that function together to optimize thermal and daylighting conditions. The unique aspect of the Responsive Skylights lies in kinetic function, human interaction, and adaptive control (the system is capable of learning daily usage pattern) under realistic operating conditions. Primary design considerations are to utilize natural daylight in the space where and when it is desired and to take optimal advantage of natural ventilation. The project builds upon existing sustainable strategies rather than defining a new definitive approach. The concept demonstrates a way of increasing the resource efficiency of a building's operation: by integrating high-level technologies into the physical built

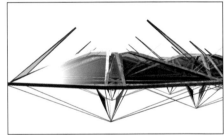

form to control the kinetic function. The approach addresses issues of energy efficiency and ways in which the environmental quality of buildings can be technologically enhanced to be more efficient and affordable, and able to reach a broader audience of users.

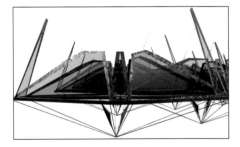

# THE MARK FISHER STUDIO

Mark Fisher is a British architect with an international reputation for the design of spectacular entertainment shows. Over the past twenty five years he has created some of the most memorable rock concerts ever staged.

His work includes *The Wall* and *Division Bell* for Pink Floyd, *Steel Wheels* and *Bridges to Babylon* for the Rolling Stones, and *Zoo TV* and *Popmart* for U2. He has worked with many other distinguished artists, including Elton John, R.E.M., Whitney Houston, Phil Collins, and Cher. He has also designed numerous one-off events and fixed installations, including "IllumiNations 25" for Walt Disney World in Orlando, Florida; "Aquamatrix," the nightly show at the Lisbon Expo'98; and the

Superbowl XXXV halftime show for MTV and the American NFL.

Fisher recently directed and designed the Millennium Show at the Dome in London. The show ran for 999 performances through the year 2000, to an audience of 6.5 million people. He also served as creative director for the Opening Celebrations at the Dome, an event that featured a cast of more than one thousand performers, including four hundred carnival artists.

The brief history of touring rock-and-roll shows outdoors began in the mid 1950s, when Colonel Parker booked Elvis Presley on a tour of U.S. baseball parks. The stages were built locally, consisting of rough-and-ready platforms with no weather covering and a rudimentary public-address system. They relied on the park facilities for lighting. This simple approach changed little during the next ten years. When the Beatles performed in New York's Shea Stadium in 1965, they played on a low platform set up on the pitcher's mound, with lighting provided by the stadium, and with the music relayed mostly through the stadium's PA system.

By 1970, the basic box—two scaffolding PA towers with a custom-built stage roof suspended between them—had become the established

# ROLLING STONES'
## *STEEL WHEELS*

form for the touring rock show. Applied decoration might camouflage the silhouette to a limited extent. But from a distance, all shows looked the same. A few bands (notably Pink Floyd in 1977, who toured with a roof of retractable umbrellas designed by Buro Happold) experimented with other roof shapes, but the possibilities for invention were always constrained by cost, because most bands did not want to end up owning a large outdoor roof at the end of a tour.

In 1989 the Rolling Stones decided to create a show that looked quite unlike anything that they, or anyone else, had toured before. The *Steel Wheels* stage design rejected the proscenium-box format of outdoor shows and explored a more narrative approach to the architecture of the structure. The underlying architectural organization of a rock concert stage—the technical requirements of sound, lighting, and weather protection, and the circulation program of backstage, stage, and audience—could not be changed. But the proscenium box was reduced to a catalog of elements that were reorganized into an expressive form.

The performance area of the stage was flanked on each side by towers of scaffolding over eighty feet high, erected by crews of up to one hundred men at a time. The top levels of the towers supported aluminum "pulley beams"— lightweight cantilever beams containing chain-pulleys that lifted the asymmetric decoration of orange girders, the lighting modules, and the thirty-foot-long cantilever tubes supporting the follow-spots into place on the facade of the structure. The bases of the scaffolding towers extended outward in a cascade of balconies, terraces, and stairs. These provided decoration at the sides of the stage and allowed the band to perform across the whole width of a stadium on different levels.

A low roof stood between the towers. The roof was visually separated from them, and it cantilevered forwards over the performance area to give efficient weather protection to the band. This reversal of the conventional form was the most recognizable statement of the design. It located the band on the dynamic central axis of a composition, rather than concealing them inside a negative space.

The sprawling composition of the Steel Wheels stage looked like a derelict steel mill. It seemed to be the antithesis of portability—an alien ruin abandoned in the triumphant sporting environment of a stadium. Its desolate form was a comment on the future of heavy industry, its seeming permanence an ironic comment on the nature of temporary architecture. It remains the largest stage ever taken on a world tour

# PINK FLOYD'S
# *DIVISION BELL*

In 1994 Mark Fisher continued his experiments with rearranging proprietary staging components, designing a 120-foot-wide arch for Pink Floyd's *Division Bell* tour. The polygonal form of the arch was assembled from straight-mast trusses, cross-braced with straight-roof trusses. The arch was built flat on a substage and lifted into place by two cranes to form a series of unfolding sections. The upstage side of the arch was filled with a curved projection surface formed using high-pressure inflatable tubes, while lighting and a 40-foot-diameter cineprojection screen were rigged inside. The band performed on a performance stage with its own cantilever roof set inside the main arch.

The use of proprietary staging components reduced the capital cost of the project. It allowed three identical main arches to be prepared for the tour without the band having to bear the cost of building the structural components. The band paid for the construction of the single perform-ance stage and the many special effects, all of which were installed inside the arch during the twenty-four hours before the show.

# U2'S
## *POPMART*

In 1992 Mark Fisher and U2 show director Willie Williams created U2's *Zoo TV* stadium tour, a production that exploited video projection technology on a massive scale to present an entertaining critique of mass-media-driven society. In 1996 they started work on the *Popmart* stage for U2. The design eclipsed the hyperbole of *Zoo TV* by presenting a parody of its excesses, based around the largest video screen that had ever been built in the world at the time (1996).

The giant video screen (one hundred and fifty feet by fifty feet) employed the newly emerging LED technology. The first LED video screens, which were assembled from individual red, green, and blue LEDs that were clustered into pixels approximately one inch in diameter, became commercially available in late 1995. For the U2 project, Fisher took the individual pixels and spaced them further apart on an open lattice grid. The pixels were mounted three inches apart on hinged panels formed from rows of folded aluminum tubes. Each panel was approximately eight feet by six feet; the panels were linked by self-locking hinges into chains that formed vertical strips of video screen fifty feet tall. The primary structure for the video screen was built from StageCo roof trusses and roof masts. The standard components were assembled into an open framework with a header truss at the top from which the strips of video screen could be lifted. The wall was stabilized by knee braces that extended upstage behind the screen and provided sup-

port for a monopitch fabric roof, which covered the technical and maintenance areas. The knee braces and the main masts of the stage were anchored to the ground by five-ton water tanks at their bases.

Each individual chain of video panels was lifted by a hoist from a header truss at the top of the screen, sliding into tracks formed from heavyweight aluminum extrusions normally used for wall cladding in StageCo stage roofs. The tracks aligned the panels and connected them to the primary structure that braced them against wind loads. The panels were stored horizontally on pallets that could be moved by forklift and rolled straight into a truck. The chains of panels folded like pages onto the pallets, alternately face-to-face and back-to-back.

This arrangement allowed the video screen elements to be assembled very quickly with a small number of people.

The bright yellow *Popmart* arch was built around a load-bearing armature of roof masts, which also supported the central audio cluster. The plastic honeycomb composite panels were attached to the masts by custom-designed

rollers mounted on their back faces. The rollers ran on heavy-duty curtain tracks that were attached to the masts at ground level before they were erected by crane. The rollers on the backs of the panels allowed the panels to be attached to the tracks at ground level and hoisted into place from above, avoiding most of the safety problems encountered in the Rolling Stones' *Voodoo Lounge* set. The cladding for the arch proceeded in parallel with the assembly of the video screen, both taking less than three hours to complete.

The Rolling Stones' 1997 *Bridges to Babylon* stage created a huge proscenium theatre at the end of the stadium, with tall theatrical curtains, ornamental columns, and other architectural elements. The primary structure was built from proprietary StageCo components, which supported the huge Sony Jumbotron video screen, the curtain tracks, the PA, and the back wall. The considerable mass of the stage structure was also used to counterweight the 150-foot-long telescoping cantilever bridge, which stretched out across the stadium to reach a B stage in the middle of the audience. The band paid for the construction of the custom-built scenery and hired the services of the staging company to erect the steelwork that supported it.

Over the past thirty years, self-deploying mechanical stage systems have been shown to save on manpower and to reduce construction time. But these systems are much smaller and less flexible than the modular systems used for the large stages illustrated here. On large projects, the economic advantage still lies with highly skilled crews assembling simple, low-tech (although efficiently engineered) components. This approach has allowed large inventories of equipment to be built up in depots around the world for relatively low costs, making it possible for the staging companies to meet the demanding logistical timetables of major world tours.

The *Popmart* and *Bridges to Babylon* stages marked the climax of a developing sequence of touring productions, which had begun with the experimental efforts of hippy entrepreneurs some thirty years before. The stages were traveling advertisements for the bands that performed on them, portable temples to the brand values of their rock-star patrons. The opportunity to build the stages was founded on the economic power of the bands, which had achieved such brand penetration of the markets in which they operated that they could guarantee to sell out stadiums anywhere in the world. They were also bands whose vision encompassed everything relating to their performance, so that they could understand the value of creating stage designs that explored their artistic ideas in an architectural way. The twenty-first century has witnessed major changes in the business that delivers popular music to the masses, and it is unlikely that such idiosyncratic conjunctions of artistic vision and commercial power will be seen in touring rock shows in the foreseeable future.

# PUGH+SCARPA

Lawrence Scarpa, AIA, and Gwynne Pugh have been practicing architecture together since forming Pugh + Scarpa in 1992. Their publications include the *Journal of Architectural Education, Metropolitan Home, Interior Design, Interiors, A+U, GA Houses, Abitare, Domus, Lotus, Architectural Review, Architectural Record, Progressive Architecture,* and *Architecture.*

In 2000 Pugh + Scarpa received over $900,000 in grants for their research and implementation of alternate energy and sustainable building strategies. In 2001 Pugh + Scarpa received six national, state, and local AIA Honor Awards, the Westside Prize for Urban Design, and the Project of the Year Award from *Interiors* magazine. In 2002 they received a national AIA design award for the second straight year. They are nearing completion of the first affordable housing project in the United States that will be one hundred percent energy neutral.

# REACTOR FILMS

The program for office and work space for Reactor Films was strategically divided into distinct areas that could be developed and detailed in phase with the construction schedule. Each programmatic element or area was explored in depth and developed in detail, presented to the client, and then dimensioned and issued to the contractor for construction. Design decisions were made in close association with the contractor and various fabricators whose expertise was fundamental to the project. A complex set of issues and relationships involving time, money, design, construction, and fabrication created a context in which the process of making and the craft of construction intensified in importance and became central aspects of the process. Construction commenced during the first week of design and permits were issued by the city by the beginning of the second week. All drawings generated for the project served as both client presentation and construction document. To facilitate this process and allow for rapid facsimile communication between participants, all drawings were completed freehand on 11-foot-by-17-inch vellum. The immediacy of working in this "one-take" or "live broadcast" context resulted in an architecture that, in essence, evolved as a drawing at full scale.

Spatially, the project revolves around a centrally located conference room, positioned to engage the public street. This room, located in the street lobby, reoccupies a used ocean-shipping container purchased from the Long

Beach shipping yard. The economic climate at the time of this project permitted the inventive reuse of this ready-made object: because of the trade imbalance with Japan, the used container was available at an extremely low cost. Like the 1930s building that this project occupies, the recycled container is transformed and perceptually repositioned to capitalize on its inherent history. In essence, it exhibits a spatial biography, its surfaces and voids charged with fragments of memory etched into it over time.

The surrounding interior space was conceived as a fluid surface wrapper rotating asymmetrically around the center of the container. This surface wrapper alternately pushes close to and peels away from the walls and structure of the existing building, suggesting a

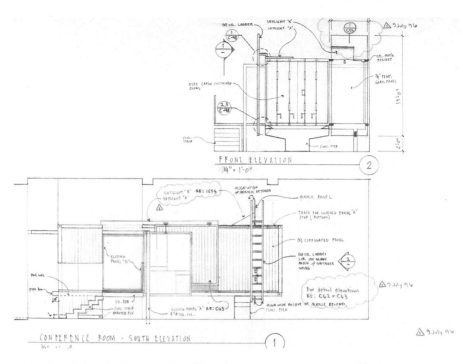

dynamic relationship between the old and new—a design attitude that respects the integrity of the former while maintaining a commitment to the generation of the inventive and thoughtful latter. Ultimately, Reactor is an attempt to stimulate meaningful experience in architecture through the process of making, questions of "how" rather than "what."

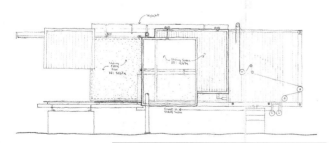

The new corporate headquarters for Davie-Brown Entertainment—a full-service entertainment marketing company with expertise in four primary areas: entertainment promotions, product placement, celebrity relations, and strategic alliances—satisfies the client's request to create a singular signature environment in which all facets of the company function under

one roof. (Formerly, the company occupied two separate office spaces, miles apart).

This project called for the renovation of ten thousand square feet in an existing industrial warehouse building in West Los Angeles. The design needed to accommodate a twenty-seven hundred square foot prop center, executive offices, staff and client offices, a conference room, product display, and a dressing room. The project was realized within extremely tight budgetary and time constraints. Occupation of the space took place only sixteen weeks after commencement of design.

The main office zone of Davie-Brown was driven by the desire to maintain a maximum amount of open space at the center of the building. This main space acts as a kind of

piazza around which all activities unfold. Visual corridors from one end of the space to the other are left unobstructed. A 20-foot-long, brilliant blue kitchen/café island sits astride one side of the space, while feature elements— a 12-foot-high hourglass-shaped, metal-clad conference room and a 14-foot-high shrink-wrapped twisting and torquing steel-frame dressing room—act as sculptural objects in an otherwise open field.

Enclosed executive offices, semienclosed staff offices, and open-landscape workstations are strategically positioned around the perimeter of the building. The primary executive offices occupy a band of previously existing offices along the front elevation. Framing remained, dropped acoustical ceilings were removed, and the offices were resurfaced with two layers of palm-sanded Plexiglas. This achieved an economy of means without a loss of effect. Light from the perimeter windows broadcasts deep into the heart of the space via the translucent wall material.

Overall, a restrained use of materials— Plexiglas, fiberglass, steel, gypsum board, and paint—created Davie-Brown Entertainment's

new headquarters. The design evolved with a desire to create a rich environment that would respond to the client's needs while also allowing the content of their work to animate the space as an integral aspect of the design.

# ACCONCI STUDIO

Born in the Bronx, New York, in 1940, Vito Acconci began his career as a fiction writer and poet, treating the page as a self-enclosed space through which the writer and reader could travel. His first work in an art context,

in the late 1960s and early 1970s, used performance, film, and video as instruments of self-analysis and person-to-person relationships. In the mid-1970s, his audio and video installations turned exhibition spaces into community meeting places. In the early 1980s, his participatory sculpture made performative spaces for viewers, whose activity resulted in the construction and deconstruction of houses. A few years later, Acconci turned to architecture, landscape architecture,

and furniture design. At the end of the 1980s, he started Acconci Studio, a group of architects who design projects for public places—streets and plazas, gardens and parks, building lobbies and transportation centers. Acconci Studio is currently composed of Vito Acconci, Dario Nuñez, Stephen Roe, Peter Dorsey, Sergio Prego, and Gia Wolff.

# MOBILE
# LINEAR CITY

When the truck is parked, a line of housing units can be pulled out of the trailer. Each unit slides on a track attached to the walls of the next larger unit, sliding out far enough so that its support legs can be folded down and fixed to the ground. The truck is driven forward so that the unit is released.

The houses are sheathed in corrugated steel; the sheathing is cut in sections, and hinges have been added so that the sections can be folded down. A gangplank folds down outside, leaving an open doorway; from under the gangplank, a ladder folds down onto the ground, allowing access to the house.

Each unit is walled off from the next; in each, the end wall is either mirrored (reflecting its own interior, and staying enclosed within itself) or translucent (giving a shadowy view into the next unit, which has a shadowy view into the next unit). Inside each house, wall panels pivot down to make a table, a bench, a bed, a shelf.

The last unit, the smallest, functions as a service unit for the entire community of houses. Inside, wall panels hinge down to provide a

stove, a refrigerator, and a toilet. Other panels fold in vertically, making stalls around the shower and the toilet. The end wall folds down to make a back porch; a ladder folds down from the wall to provide access to the services of the city.

The floors of each unit are steel grating, underneath, a fluorescent light at the back of each house casts light from below, across the floor. The city is public; people can walk underneath each unit and look up into it—unless the inhabitant intervenes and lays a rug down on the floor. The more you use the service unit, the less private it becomes; you can fold down a wall, for example, and use the toilet it provides, but now your ass is exposed to the world outside.

Designed by Vito Acconci with Luis Vera and Jenny Schrider.

# CAR HOTEL

This project involves a conventional car, converted from carriage of passengers to storage of freight. The driver's seat remains unencumbered; the rest of the car is filled with equipment and machinery.

In the middle of the car is a hydraulic piston; attached to this are stackable beds/seat units. A hydraulic pump is stored in the trunk.

The shell of the car is separated and lifted, hydraulically, off its floor. The shell functions as the roof of a four-story hotel. Each floor consists of a bed made out of rubber for outdoor use; each bed is formed into a pillow at the head and a seat at the foot. Next to each seat is a television, directed toward the floor below. A chain ladder rolls up off a spool at the floor of the car, allowing access to the stories above.

The car is driven through the city, from place to place, from neighborhood to neighborhood, providing a mobile hotel unit whenever one is needed, whenever one is wanted.

Designed by Vito Acconci with Luis Vera, Jenny Schrider, Charles Doherty, and Christina Arn.

A plane of sand passes through the car: it sits on the hood, it fills the inside of the cab in an L-shape (leaving room for the driver), it cantilevers out from the trunk. The container of the sand is a thin, transparent box; its frame is mirrored stainless steel, reflecting a sliver of what is outside. The hood and the trunk can still be opened with the plane of sand attached. The sand is loose inside its container. The plane is only three-quarters filled with sand, which shifts as the car moves.

Coming up through the sand are six televisions, planted in clusters: two small TV's over the end of the hood; three TV's, big and small, inside the car (the big TV cuts through the roof); and one big TV cantilevered out from the trunk. The televisions are embedded at different angles, with the screens facing different directions; the screens do not have to be seen. There is no need for sound; the TV's are used as the rocks of a Japanese garden. The televisions show conventional channels, broadcast television. The programs change, hour by hour, day by day, but the programming stays the same.

As you drive the car, you are sitting in the middle of a Japanese garden. If you are standing on the sidewalk, the Japanese garden passes you like a ship in the night. If you are in another car, you might try to keep up with the garden—you are trailing it, it is right beside you, neck and neck, it is in view but just out of reach, until it turns the corner and disappears like a ghost.

Designed by Vito Acconci with Luis Vera, Jenny Schrider, Charles Doherty, and Jean Hahn.

JAPANESE CAR GARDEN

# WORLD IN YOUR BONES

The understructure of this microenvironment is screwed into your bones like a prosthetic skeleton. It lives on your back, on your limbs, on your head; it moves as you move, and you barely notice it as you go about your business. When you feel some need, the plot thickens: the tubes slide, pivot, telescope out—you become your own chair, your own bed, your own

vehicle. A microshell fans out over your head: your head becomes your office. A macroshell fans out over your body: your body becomes your house. Visitors enter your house as if coming in under your clothes. Your house leeches onto a building: you own your own apartment, and you move your apartment from building to building. Your house leeches

onto a plane, a train, a ship, a car: you ride free of charge.

The operation was a success: not only is the patient alive, the patient wakes up twice the man he used to be.

Designed by Vito Acconci with Luis Vera, Dario Nuñez, Azarahksh Damood, and Tomas King.

On land, a rowboat is sunk into the ground. Its bow is filled with soil and grass, a tree grows out of the bow, and the oars are embedded in the ground as if rowing on land. You can step down into the boat and sit inside, as if the land were water.

Facing this boat, in the water, is its mirror image: a rowboat wedged into a circular plane of grass. The rowboat combines with the grass: as in the rowboat on shore, its bow is filled with soil and grass, and a tree grows out of the bow.

You can step out onto the grass plane, or step into the boat and row. The boat takes with it the circular plane of grass, pulling out of a semicircular cut in the shore, so you can row your island out to sea.

Designed by Vito Acconci with Luis Vera, Jenny Schrider, and Lisa Albin.

PERSONAL ISLAND

# OFFICE OF MOBILE DESIGN

Since 1998, Office of Mobile Design (OMD) has focused on developing mobile architecture, designing and constructing portable, demountable, and mobile structures. OMD specializes in finding nonstandard solutions to unconventional and unique problems, with dynamic rather than static and permanent structures. A majority of OMD's work involves providing services to public agencies, nonprofit agencies, museums, schools, commercial businesses, and private interests.

Jennifer Siegal, principal-owner of OMD, received a Master of Architecture degree from Southern California Institute of Architecture. She is currently an associate professor of architecture at Woodbury University, Los Angeles. She was awarded an AIA Honorable Mention in 1998, the Association of Collegiate Schools of Architecture's Faculty Design Award in 2000 and their Collaborative Practice Award in 1999 and 2000. In 2001 she was named an Emerging Voice in Design by *Architectural Record*. In 2003 her work will be exhibited at the National Design Triennial at the Cooper-Hewitt National Design Museum Smithsonian Institution and at the "Out of the Ordinary" exhibition at the Walker Art Center.

# PORTABLE HOUSE

Harkening back to prehistoric models of shelter and dwelling, the Portable House adapts, relocates, and reorients itself to accommodate an ever-changing environment. It offers an ecosensitive and economical alternative to the increasingly expensive permanent structures that constitute most of today's housing options. At the same time, the Portable House calls into question preconceived notions of the trailer home and trailer park, creating an entirely new option for those with disposable income but insufficient resources for entering the conventional housing market.

The Portable House's expandable/contractible spaces, the varying degrees of translucency of its materials, and its very portability render it uniquely flexible and adaptable. Its central kitchen/bath core divides and separates the sleeping space from the eating/living space in a compact assemblage of form and function. When additional space is required, the living-room structure can be extended outward to increase square footage. By design, the house can be maneuvered and reoriented to take advantage of natural light and airflow.

As an entity unto itself, the Portable House adapts to or creates new social dynamics wherever it goes. For example, when individually owned units are grouped together, they can create common spaces for social interactions, such as gardens, courtyards, and side yards, or multiple units can be arranged by one owner to create separate but adjacent spaces for living, working, and socializing.

The Portable House's mobility, the way it moves across and rests lightly upon the landscape, provides a provocative counterpoint to the status quo housing model. It recalls a time when the elements that constituted shelter were easily manipulated to accommodate innumerable variables and conditions. It likewise offers flexibility in the sociodynamics of everyday living. Whether momentarily located in the open landscape, briefly situated in an urban space, or positioned for a more lengthy stay, the Portable House accommodates a wide range of needs and functions.

# MOBILE ECO LAB

The Mobile Eco Lab was built in collaboration with the Hollywood Beautification Team, a grassroots group founded with the mission to restore beauty and integrity to Los Angeles's Hollywood community. Verbal and visual exchanges took place using computer-animated drawings, traditional drafting, and large-scale modeling techniques. Full-scale work was performed with a defined material palette, specifically that of a donated cargo trailer and cast-offs from film sets. The 8-by-35-foot trailer now travels throughout Los Angeles County to inform K–12 schoolchildren about the importance of saving and protecting our planet. Like a circus tent, this mobile icon arrives at the schoolyard, where the lab's elevated walkways fold down and slide out of the trailer's body. It is immediately recognizable as a place for interaction, discovery, and fun.

As a working mobile classroom, the Eco Lab provides a base for a range of exhibitions—all of which focus on ecology. Arriving at the threshold of the trailer, a child climbs up a set of folding stairs that has been lowered by a nautical winch. When the stairway meets the ground, the attached springs and wheels swivel into place, absorb the compression, and provide access. Ascending the recycled expanded steel treads, the child enters a multimedia antechamber. The chamber facilitates learning by providing a computer for surfing the Internet on topics focusing on ecology. The young visitors hear a video describing a tree's growth cycle. Each child is then given a small container and a tree sapling to care for. Moving single file, the visitors emerge from the trailer onto a fold-down, tiered catwalk. As they advance, they move back into the body of the trailer, and reemerge outside onto a stage-like platform that rolls out of the wheel wells. Here the children water their saplings and the teacher uses this space to discuss each child's role in planting trees and maintaining a sustainable environment. Progressing to the core of the Eco Lab, visitors gather in the dappled light streaming through the woven wooden wall. The floor, engraved with a giant California oak leaf encircled by the words "you are ecology," provides the space for discussion and questions.

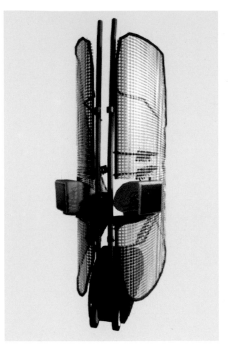

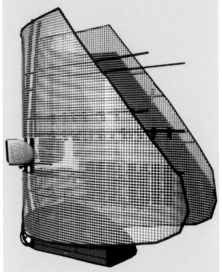

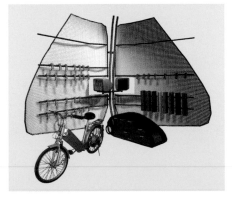

The firm ZVO is a rising star in the rapidly expanding field of zero emissions vehicle (ZEV) design and manufacture. Its designs for electric bicycles have garnered praise from ecological groups and industrial designers alike.

The Zevos Kiosk is a lifestyle-driven apparel and merchandising center. This portable, flexible "store within a store" offers a retail and service hub ideal for placement in university student centers, shopping malls, and airports—or anywhere else people gather for commerce and socializing.

The nature of the Zevos Kiosk allows for wide-ranging flexibility of use. It moves about easily on its wheeled base, which doubles as a securable ZVO bicycle repair and service station. The wings of its main structure can pivot open to reveal a simple and interchangeable display system for ZVO bicycle accessories: portable palm-held computer units, saddlebags for laptop computers, alternative-colored battery cartridges, and cyclometers. Computer monitors mounted on hinged support posts swivel about, offering views from varying directions. Whether the kiosk is open for business with its wings spread wide, or closed securely during off hours, these monitors run educational, informational, or promotional consumer programming.

The dramatic profile of the Zevos Kiosk evokes a sailboat at full mast, or a graceful butterfly. With its striking form and originality, it is an instant attention-grabber. What is more, its iconographic folding screenlike structure, made of lightweight materials, doubles as a billboard. With a clear display of product and logo, the Zevos Kiosk proclaims its purpose and wares wherever it travels—a unique, compact, all-purpose combination of marketing tool, product display, retail, technology access, and consumer information.

ZEVOS KIOSK

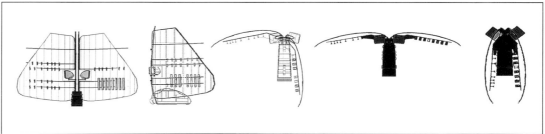

# PORTABLE CONSTRUCTION TRAINING CENTER

The Portable Construction Training Center (PCTC) was conceived for the Venice Community Housing Corporation, an organization founded with the mission to develop and maintain permanently affordable housing for disadvantaged and low-income individuals. This non-profit organization affords an opportunity for their student trainees to learn construction skills and in turn apply those skills to needed projects. The 14-by-65-foot PCTC is a hands-on classroom used as the focal point in this construction training process. The PCTC allows space for the four basic construction trades: plumbing, painting and plaster repair, carpentry, and electrical.

The design concept encourages visual connections between apprentice and teacher. A

14-by-14-foot meeting space at the PCTC's threshold exhibits construction example boards and provides a well-lit location to gather between building sessions. Like a large porch, one entire length of the trailer folds open to reveal interior independent workstations. This creates a catwalk for the teachers, which facilitates inspection and interaction. In this 90-degree position, the operable translucent panels give shade and regulate the natural flow of hot and cool air. Additionally, the far end of the PCTC folds open to provide a wood shop where tools can be disengaged to roll outside beyond the parameter of the trailer.

Portable, flexible, and operable, the PCTC is a symbol for alternative construction techniques and provides a place to teach those techniques. Designed with Pugh+Scarpa, Los Angeles and Woodbury University design/build students.

OFFICE OF MOBILE DESIGN
PORTABLE CONSTRUCTION TRAINING CENTER 117

Fold out. Plug in. Boot up. The iMobile is a roving online portal for accessing the global communications networks and announcing the latest computer systems, peripherals, hardware, and software. Its six individual workpods are outfitted with complete computer set-ups, programmable and adaptable as needed for new product promotion or sampling.

Marvel at the remarkable efficiency of a dynamic mobile enterprise. The iMobile gathers up the information superhighway and rolls it out along our everyday streets and roads. It is here that the workplace effortlessly evolves, enabling businesses to respond to the need for augmentation, contraction, and metamorphosis. The iMobile offers building solutions to the

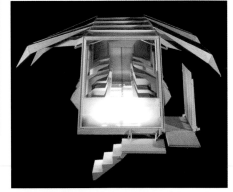

# iMOBILE

The iMobile represents the future standard of specialized, multipurpose consumer-directed marketing and customer service. With its striking, dramatic design, the iMobile combines forces with existing innovative products that have become iconographic emblems of new technologies. Wherever it travels, the iMobile is a unique marketing device—a recognizable, self-contained promotional unit that unfolds before your eyes and invites you to come on in, have a seat, and take a spin.

mobile entrepreneur. Based on an economy of movement, where form follows necessity, this adaptable and flexible structure is always responsive to its immediate and shifting environment. Composed and durably constructed from high-quality, light, and affordable materials, this self-sufficient and relocatable structure gives shape to the metropolis of the future.

The iMobile goes anywhere. It is a mobile store, bringing the shopping experience directly to the consumer—whether parked in commercial parking lots, visiting neighborhoods with limited computer access, creating a scene at outdoor public events, or participating in industry conventions (iMobile rolls right into the convention venue, an instant promotional display unit!).

# MOBILE EVENT CITY ARCHITECTURE

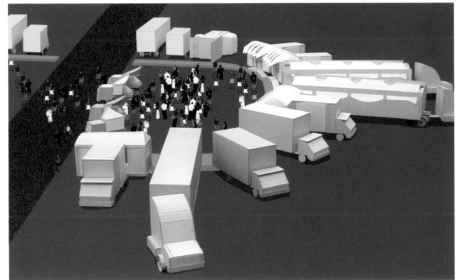

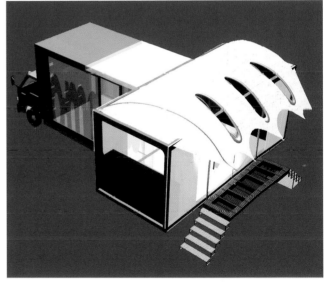

The Mobile Event City Architecture (MECA) provides an overall upgrade of event facilities for a socially conscious event-planning firm that creates multiday outdoor charity events in support of AIDS, breast cancer, world hunger, and like causes. The goal is to provide structures for their nightly encampments that are easily relocatable, adaptable to varying site conditions, climate controlled, clean, well lit, and visually striking—and that help engender intimate social interaction.

Four possible master-plan schemes assemble the campsite components into a four-tiered hierarchy, which can then be organized either around a central gathering space (Town Square), along a linear corridor (Main Street), or in a combination thereof.

Individual campsite elements, such as Medical Services, Outreach (marketing), Vending Kiosks, and the "Remembrance Place," use existing truck types as points of departure, then hybridize them with tensile fabric structures. These compact, self-contained mobile structures are weather resistant, hygienic, and easy to deploy and relocate. As they unfold, slide open, pivot, and pull apart to expand their floor areas, their fabric components take shape to form roofs, walls, and overhangs, transforming their host vehicles into unique, wondrous building/machines.

The master plans call for the primary structures to be situated along an elevated boardwalk that either extends linearly along Main Street or circumscribes the Town Square. This raised thoroughfare, composed of sections that slide out of each vehicle and interlock, unifies the disparate elements to the Mobile City, providing identifiable and accessible circulation that is also a level alternative to an often uneven ground plane. This streamlines the organization of campsite operations and augments the overall level of comfort and care afforded to event participants.

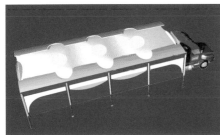

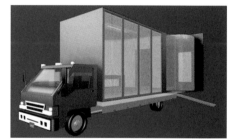

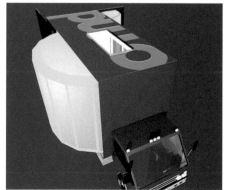